5/99

Natu
and
wort

13

For tho
feng sh
harmor
you car
home t
tentme
feng sh

If yo
in roon
door lo
existing
ing neg
situati
Put fe
the ha

About the Author

Richard Webster was born in New Zealand in 1946, where he still resides. He travels widely every year, lecturing and conducting workshops on psychic subjects around the world. He has written many books, mainly on psychic subjects, and also writes monthly magazine columns.

Richard is married with three children. His family is very supportive of his occupation, but his oldest son, after watching his father's career, has decided to become an accountant.

To Write to the Author

If you wish to contact the author or would like more information about this book, please write to the author in care of Llewellyn Worldwide, and we will forward your request. Both the author and publisher appreciate hearing from you. Llewellyn Worldwide cannot guarantee that every letter written to the author can be answered, but all will be forwarded. Please write to:

Richard Webster
℅ Llewellyn Worldwide
P.O. Box 64383, Dept. K809-5
St. Paul, MN 55164-0383, U.S.A.

Please enclose a self-addressed, stamped envelope for reply, or $1.00 to cover costs. If outside the U.S.A., enclose international postal reply coupon.

101
FENG SHUI
TIPS

for

the

Home

RICHARD
WEBSTER

1999
Llewellyn Publications
St. Paul, Minnesota 55164-0383
U.S.A.

FIRST EDITION
Third printing, 1999

Cover design: Tom Grewe
Calligraphic cover graphic: Nakaseko Tamami
Interior illustrations: Carla Shale and Jeannie Ferguson
Book design: Amy Rost
Editing and typesetting: Laura Gudbaur
Project management: Michael Maupin

Library of Congress Cataloging-in-Publication Data
Webster, Richard, 1946–
   101 Feng Shui Tips for the Home / Richard Webster
   p. cm.
   Includes index.
   ISBN 1-56718-809-5 (pbk.)
   1. Feng-shui. I. Title.
   BF1779.F4W42 1998
   133.3'337—dc21   98-9695
                                  CIP

Llewellyn Worldwide does not participate in, endorse, or have any authority or responsibility concerning private business transactions between our authors and the public.

   All mail addressed to the author is forwarded but the publisher cannot, unless specifically instructed by the author, give out an address or phone number.

Llewellyn Publications
A Division of Llewellyn Worldwide, Ltd.
P.O. Box 64383, Dept. K809-5
St. Paul, Minnesota 55164-0383

Printed in the United States of America

Other Books by Richard Webster

Dedication

For Chuck and Betsy Hickock.

Acknowledgments

I would like to express my grateful thanks
to T'ai Lau for his help and advice.

Contents

Introduction

*First comes destiny, and then comes luck. Third comes feng
shui, which is followed by philanthropy and education.*
        —ancient Chinese saying

Feng shui literally means "wind and water." Some five
thousand years ago the ancient Chinese believed that if you
sited your home in the right location you would lead a life
of contentment, happiness, and abundance. Naturally, we
all want to lead happy, successful lives, and anything that
can help us achieve these aims is well worth investigation.

The term "feng shui" is a comparatively modern one.
The original Chinese characters for feng shui were *Ham* and
Yu. Ham means receiving energy from the heavens, while
Yu connects the earth to the rest of the heavenly bodies.[1]
Consequently, feng shui began as an attempt to connect
heaven and earth.

No one knows exactly when the practice of feng shui
began. In China they have a charming story about its origin

that may or may not be true. Wu, the first of the three legendary emperors of Chinese prehistory, was involved in irrigation work on the Yellow River. One day, he and his workers saw a large tortoise crawl out of the river. This was considered a good omen as in those days they believed that gods lived inside the shells of turtles and tortoises. However, this tortoise was especially auspicious, because the markings on its shell created a perfect magic square. Wu gathered all his wise men together, and they studied this strange phenomenon for a long while. Ultimately, this magic square was to become the basis of feng shui, the I Ching, Chinese astrology, and Chinese numerology.

Over the centuries, by a process of observation and meditation, feng shui evolved. For the first two and a half thousand years of its history, feng shui was largely a geographic evaluation of the landscape. This became known as the **Form School** of feng shui. It became much more personalized after the invention of the compass, some twenty-three hundred years ago, when the **Compass School** was formed. This major advance allowed feng shui practitioners to choose the correct placements of people's homes based on their dates of birth. Today, there are many variations of feng shui, but they can still be categorized as being part of either the Form or Compass School.

Nowadays, we are much more aware of the effects that our environment has upon us. It makes good sense to use feng shui to improve our home environment, as it allows us and our loved ones to enjoy more harmony, balance, and success in our lives. By studying this book and putting the ideas into practice, you and your loved ones will gain all of these benefits.

1

Feng Shui in the Home

A home should be much more than just a place to rest our head at night. The word home conjures up many more pleasant images in our mind than the words *house* or *apartment*. When you return from work, does it feel good to be home? Do you start to get this feeling as you come up the street, or into the drive? If so, you already have a great deal of positive feng shui in your home.

The moment we move into a new home we invest it with our personalities. Every piece of furniture has a story to tell. Ornaments and pictures on the walls reflect our tastes and attitudes. The books on the bookshelves reveal our interests. Framed photographs remind us of the people we love and also tell others a great deal about our backgrounds and the people we care about. Even when we move into a temporary home for just a few weeks, we try to make it as pleasing as possible by displaying personal objects that give us pleasure.

Consequently, by making their homes as harmonious and as comfortable as possible, most people intuitively use feng shui all the time without knowing it. I am sure you have had the experience of walking into a room and subconsciously feeling that everything was right. You have doubtless also had the experience of entering a room and sensing that something was wrong. In the first case, the feng shui of the room was good. Most of the time, the second room would also experience good feng shui with just a few simple adjustments.

Ch'i

The ancient Chinese believed that a green dragon or white tiger lived beneath every hill or mountain. Where these two animals symbolically coupled was the perfect location for a home. They also believed that the dragon created **ch'i** with its breath. In fact, ch'i is often referred to as "the dragon's breath."

Ch'i is the universal life force. It gathers near gently flowing water and is created whenever anything is done perfectly. A composer creating a beautiful melody is also creating ch'i. A poet writing a sonnet creates ch'i, too. Someone baking a magnificent cake is creating ch'i. A tennis player scoring an ace is creating ch'i.

To operate effectively we need to encourage as much ch'i as possible into our home.

Ch'i can be both positive and negative. For instance, gently moving water creates positive ch'i, while stagnant water creates negative ch'i. We want as much good ch'i as possible, but naturally want to eliminate any negative ch'i.

Ch'i needs to be nurtured and gathered. It is easily scattered and dissipated by strong winds or rapidly flowing water. This is why we want gentle breezes and meandering streams near our homes. Both combine to create good, positive ch'i.

Yin and Yang

Ch'i is made up of both **yin** and **yang**. Yin and yang are the two opposites in the universe. For instance, night and day, short and tall, front and back, and male and female are all examples of yin and yang. None of these can exist without the other. Without night there could be no day, and without black there would be no white. The ancients never tried to define yin and yang, but delighted in collecting lists of opposites.[1]

Yin is represented by black, and yang is white. The concept began many thousands of years ago when the ancient Chinese called the shady, northern slopes of a mountain yin and the sunny, southern slopes yang.

As a result of this, the ancient Taoists used the familiar symbol of yin and yang to represent completion. This symbol, which looks like two tadpoles in a circle, symbolizes

Figure 1A

the universe (Figure 1A). One tadpole is black with a white dot in it, and the other white with a black dot in it. The dots indicate that inside every yin there is a certain amount of yang, and inside every yang is a degree of yin.

Everything in the universe is composed of yin and yang energies that are constantly interacting with each other.

In our own environments, we need a balance of yin and yang. If our neighborhood is entirely flat, it is said to be too yin. If it is extremely hilly, it is considered too yang. Thousands of years ago, hills were used to represent the yang energies. Nowadays, we usually look at neighboring houses to provide this. It is interesting to reflect that pagodas (Figure 1B) were originally devised to create yang energy. Today, miniature pagodas are often still used as decorative ornaments and to symbolize the yang energies.

Figure 1B

If your property is too yin, you can remedy this by planting shrubs and trees or perhaps introducing rocks or a garden shed. It is important to think ahead. Small trees frequently grow into big trees, which can alter the feng shui of the immediate area.

If your area is too yang, you may be able to flatten part of your property to create a balance of yin and yang energy.

Even the house itself is divided into yin and yang areas. The front of the house, which serves to greet people to the property, is outgoing and yang. The farther inside the house you go, the more yin, and private, the rooms become. This is why bedrooms usually feel better if they are situated well away from the front door.

The Five Elements

In feng shui we use the traditional **five elements** of Chinese astrology: wood, fire, earth, metal, and water. The Chinese believe that everything in the universe belongs to one of these five elements. They represent the five different ways that ch'i energy is manifested. Your year of birth determines which of these elements is most important to you. Elements for each year of birth are listed in Appendix 1. In fact, if you have a Chinese horoscope prepared, you will find that you have most or all five of these elements in your makeup. A good astrologer will be able to balance and interpret the different weightings of each element in your horoscope.

The five elements proceed in a definite progression. Wood burns and creates fire. After fire has burned out, the result is earth. From the earth we obtain metal (gold, silver, etc.). Metal liquefies which symbolically produces water. Finally, water nurtures which creates wood (plants). Consequently, we have a circle of energy that continually goes around and around (Figure 1C).

The five elements also relate to different shapes. Fire is triangular, earth is square, metal is round, water is horizontal and curving, and wood is rectangular and vertical. Architects make use of this when they want to design a building for a specific purpose. A building designed to deal with financial projects will often be metal-shaped.

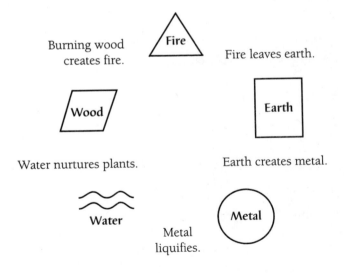

Burning wood creates fire. / Fire / Fire leaves earth.

Wood

Earth

Water nurtures plants.

Water

Metal liquifies.

Metal

Earth creates metal.

Figure 1C

Wood

Color	Green
Season	Spring
Direction	East
Shape	Rectangular and vertical
Animal	Dragon
Virtue	Benevolence
Quality	Loyalty

Wood is creative. If this is the predominant element in your makeup, you will need to express yourself in some way, ideally creatively. Wood nurtures others and represents humanitarianism, strong family ties, and new ideas.

Live plants, fresh flowers, and green objects represent the wood element.

The Bank of China building in Hong Kong is a spectacular and controversial example of a wood-shaped building.

Fire

Color	Red
Season	Summer
Direction	South
Shape	Triangular
Animal	Phoenix
Virtue	Propriety
Quality	Reason and logic

Fire gives enthusiasm and energy. Consequently, fire people make natural leaders. It is associated with fame and good fortune. However, fire not only warms and invigorates; it can also burn. People with the right amount of fire in their makeup are fair, considerate, and honorable. People with too much fire are critical, foul-mouthed, and resentful of other people's success.

Candlesticks, incense holders, and red objects represent the fire element.

The pyramid that forms the entrance to the Louvre is an excellent example of a fire-shaped structure. It is in striking juxtaposition to the water-shaped building of the Louvre. Together, they create enormous power and energy that attracts tourists from all around the world.

Earth

Color	Yellow
Season	Indian summer
Direction	Center
Shape	Square
Animal	Ox
Virtue	Faith
Quality	Honesty

Earth gives stability, reliability, and common sense. It is patient, honest, loyal, methodical, and well-balanced. Earth people are sympathetic and responsible. However, the earth element can also be over-demanding and unwilling to make changes or progress.

Yellow objects and any items made of terra-cotta, pottery, or ceramics serve to represent the earth element.

Most homes are reasonably squarish in shape, which means that they are described as earth homes.

Metal

Color	White (and metallic colors such as gold)
Season	Autumn
Direction	West
Shape	Round
Animal	Tiger
Virtue	Righteousness
Quality	Clarity of thought

Metal is the element of business and financial success. It represents clear thinking and an upright, moral outlook. However, metal can also indicate a knife or sword, which shows that metal can also be violent. This can be expressed through emotional outbursts and a lack of focus.

Wind chimes and anything else made of metal represent the metal element.

The round dome on the top of the Taj Mahal makes it a fine example of a metal-shaped building.

Water

Color	Black and blue
Season	Winter
Direction	North
Shape	Horizontal and curving
Animal	Tortoise
Virtue	Wisdom
Quality	Persistence

Water symbolizes knowledge, wisdom, communication, and travel. Water can be either gentle (soft rain) or violent (hurricanes). Water is essential for life on earth and nourishes all living things. However, water can also wear away the hardest rock.

A fish bowl, decorative fountain, or anything else that is black, blue, or contains water represents the water element.

The Houses of Parliament in London are a good example of a water-shaped building.

Shars

Shars are frequently known as "poison arrows." They are created by straight lines or sharp angles. A road heading in a straight line towards your home is creating a shar (Figure 1D, next page). A similar shar may also be caused by the path leading to your front door if it is a straight line.

Nearby houses can also create shars. If the house next door to you is at a forty-five degree angle to your home, it is likely to be sending a shar towards you (Figure 1E). Roof lines can also send shars in your direction.

Fortunately, in feng shui there is a remedy for every negative thing, including shars. If the shar cannot be seen, it ceases to exist. Consequently, a hedge, fence or tree can be used to conceal the shar and effectively eliminate it.

Mirrors can also be used as a remedy. The perfect mirror is a circular one, approximately one to two inches in diameter, centered in the middle of an octagonal shaped piece of wood. Around the mirror are the **eight trigrams** of the I Ching. (The trigrams are discussed in the next chapter.) The trigrams are important as they make the mirror active, rather than passive. These active mirrors are known as **pa-kua mirrors**.

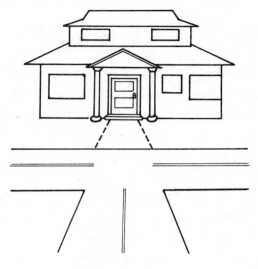

Figure 1D

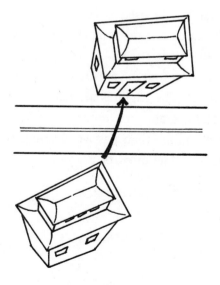

Figure 1E

The mirror is placed on the side of the house pointing directly at the shar. Symbolically, the mirror reflects the shar back where it came from.

The people of Hong Kong often have "mirror wars." Someone will see a shar heading towards him and will erect a pa-kua mirror to send it back. His neighbor will notice the mirror and will erect one of his own. Before long, they will have several mirrors each, effectively sending the shar back and forth.

Feng Shui Tips

1. Use your intuition when it comes to arranging furniture and ornaments. You will almost always make the right choice according to feng shui.

2. Try to have all five elements represented in your home. Together they symbolize completion and help create a sense of harmony and comfort.

3. Your furniture should represent both yin (curved) and yang (straight). A combination of gentle curves and straight lines helps create balance.

4. Mirrors are useful for reflecting back shars, and can also reflect people and pleasant views from outside. Mirrors should be kept as clean as possible to help the ch'i flow freely.

5. Chandeliers are a wonderful way of attracting ch'i into your home. The different crystals draw in the ch'i and then reflect it out again in every direction.

6. Crystals and bright objects also reflect ch'i energy outwards. Keep any reflective surfaces clean to encourage the ch'i.

7. Make sure your home is kept in the best possible condition. Keep the paint work fresh, repair any leaking faucets, and replace any blown bulbs as quickly as possible. Keep your windows clean and replace any cracked or broken glass. This is because the health of your home relates directly to you and your health.

2

Evaluating Your Home

In this chapter we will look at two methods of evaluating your home. The first is known as the **Aspirations of the Pa-kua**. This is a simple and convenient method that does not require a compass. Because it is easy to do, you will soon find yourself doing it automatically whenever you walk into someone's home. The second method, known as the **Nine Stars**, is more complicated and requires a compass. It also takes practice to become good at it, but you will find it extremely helpful and well worth the small investment of time and energy to master. In practice, I use both methods.

Shape of Your Home

In feng shui, square or oblong houses are more desirable than unusual shapes. For instance, an L-shaped house symbolizes a meat cleaver, which is certainly not desirable.

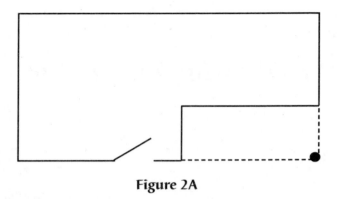

Figure 2A

Fortunately, there are remedies for every possible shape. The remedy for an L-shaped house is to place a light on a pole in the garden to symbolically complete the house and make it appear rectangular (Figure 2A). Other remedies are to plant shrubs or erect a low wall to symbolically complete the house.

Aspirations of the Pa-kua

The pa-kua (pronounced "par-kwar") is an octagonal-shaped symbol of Chinese culture. Each side represents a direction and an important area of life. The pa-kua can be placed over a plan of your house, or a single room, and can even be used on something as small as a desk (Figure 2B).

For convenience sake, the pa-kua is often shown inside a three-by-three square. If your home is square or

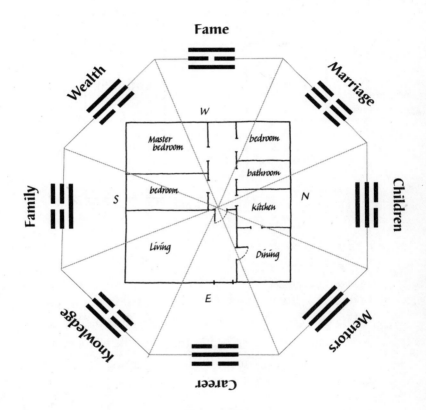

Figure 2B

Wealth	Fame	Marriage
Family		Children
Knowledge	Career	Mentors

Figure 2C

rectangular, the pa-kua can be overlaid on top of it easily (Figure 2C). If your home is more unusual in shape, the pa-kua may cover part of the garden as well as the house. Unless remedied, this indicates that your life is not completely balanced. Figure 2D shows a house lacking a Wealth area. (Notice that the pa-kua has been "stretched" to accomodate the rectangular shape of the house.) The people in this house would find this area of their life restricted until this problem was remedied. Figure 2E shows a house that is missing the Fame area. The standing in the community of the people who live in this house will increase as soon as they rectify this difficulty.

Remember though, that even if part of your house is not covered entirely by the pa-kua, you are not completely

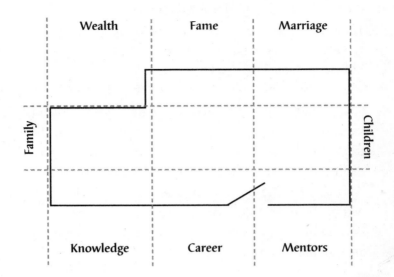

Figure 2D

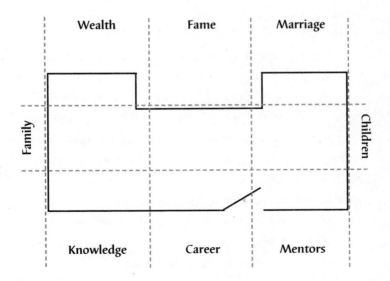

Figure 2E

missing that aspect, as the pa-kua is also placed over each individual room.

The side of the pa-kua that covers Knowledge, Career, and Mentors is placed on the side of the house that your front door is situated on. For feng shui purposes, the front door is the door you use most frequently, or your main entrance. This means that if you walk in your front door and go as far as you can diagonally to the left, you will find yourself in the Wealth area of your home.

Each area of your home represents one of the eight areas of life.

Wealth

The Wealth area naturally governs money, but it also relates to anything that makes your life richer. If you need more money, this area of your home can be activated by encouraging more ch'i to it. There are many ways of doing this. You may increase the amount of light in this part of the house. A mirror, chandelier, or hanging crystal will all help encourage more ch'i. Because water means wealth in feng shui, an aquarium or small fountain would prove helpful in activating this area. Metal objects will also prove beneficial. In the East, it is common to hang coins on the wall to act as a silent affirmation to encourage more money. A friend of mine has increased his net worth several times over since he began displaying a beautiful silver tea service in the wealth area of his home.

Fame

Next to Wealth is the Fame area. This represents your standing in the community. If you want to become better known in the community you live in, you need to activate this area. This area also represents who you really are. We all have goals and dreams. You can encourage these by displaying items in this part of the house that will inspire you to action. Encourage more ch'i, of course, by increasing the light into this part of the house. You may also display trophies, awards and pictures of yourself to enhance the qualities that you desire. You may also display items that you find personally attractive. Use items of the finest quality that you can afford. A round mirror is very beneficial in the Fame area.

Marriage

The Marriage area relates specifically to close relationships. This is usually a personal relationship, but you can activate this area to encourage business relationships as well. If you are looking for a new relationship, or want to improve the relationship you are already in, you need to activate this area of your home. Increase the ch'i by increasing the amount of light in this part of the house. Display wedding photographs and any other objects that you consider romantic. A painting or photograph of two lovers walking hand in hand can do wonders for this part of your life. An acquaintance of mine placed two candlesticks in this location of her home. After being on her own for eight years, she found a new life partner in less than two months. She still lights her candles every night to keep the love alive.

Family

The Family area means family in a wide sense of the word. It includes all the people you care about and love. This area is a good place to display family portraits, bronzed baby shoes, and family awards. Inherited items, such as antique furniture or a family Bible, all serve to stimulate the Family area and contribute to feelings of continuity. However, it is important that you find these inherited items attractive. It is bad feng shui to display items that you do not like. The Family area also relates to health. If you, or someone you care about, is ill, this area should be activated by using crystals or additional light.

Children

The Children area relates mainly to your children, but also includes creativity. If you want children, or are having problems with your children, you should activate this area of your home. This is also a good place to display photographs of your children and to display artwork that they have produced. In this area, you can also store toys and other objects that are special to your children. This is a good area for creative work. A desk placed here would provide an excellent place to work on any creative interest. An artist I know keeps his stereo system in this part of the house, even though he works in the Fame area. He says that the sound of music coming from the Children area enhances his creativity.

Knowledge

The Knowledge area relates to spirituality and learning. It is a good place for bookshelves, and could not be bettered as a study area. This area should be activated if you, or anyone in the family, is involved with study of any kind. A painting in this area showing high mountains and a river or waterfall can symbolize your unlimited potential. Glassware, especially crystal, can serve to place you in closer contact with your spiritual self.

Career

The Career area is a good place for a home office. It should be activated if you are trying to progress in your career. It is a good place for a fax machine, computer or anything else that relates to your career. This area can be activated by displaying a mirror, wind chimes and an attractive table lamp.

In the East, it is common to have affirmations, drawn in beautiful calligraphy, on the walls. These affirmations look like works of art and remind the occupants of where they are heading in their careers. A man I know did not want to hang affirmations on the wall, but instead keeps a photograph album in this area of his house. In the album are displayed photographs of where he wants to go in his career. He credits the photograph album with a series of rapid promotions he has enjoyed in his career.

Mentors

The Mentors area relates to people who can help you. If you wish to attract someone like this into your life, you can activate this area by hanging a crystal. For many people, mentors relate to spiritual help. Consequently, this is a good place to display anything that relates to your faith or philosophy in life. This part of the house also relates to travel. Again, activate this area if you have dreams of traveling, especially travel overseas.

These areas spread out beyond the home indefinitely. If you are wanting to become famous and make a name for yourself, you should seek these things in the direction indicated by the placement of the Fame area. Likewise, the best direction for a school or college is in the direction indicated by the Knowledge area. If you are trying to find a new relationship, the best direction is the one indicated by Marriage.

Confusions can arise, though. You may be happy in your job and have good prospects for the future, but the place where you work may not be in the direction indicated by the Career area. In this instance, you should head off to work in the morning by driving in the Career direction for half a mile or so, and then turn back and head to work. This means that you are symbolically heading in the Career direction.

I have an acquaintance who is fortunate enough to have an apartment overlooking the ocean.

"I can't find a relationship," he told me a year ago. "My Marriage direction is on the other side of the ocean!"

This is not really the case. I told him to walk down to the seashore, then return and head off in any direction he chose. This meant that he symbolically started his quest by heading in the right direction. Incidentally, within six months of doing this he met someone, and they are now engaged.

"I was about to give up," he told me. "It seemed silly walking down to the beach every morning, but it became a habit. I'm glad I stuck with it!"

Clutter

In feng shui, clutter should be avoided as much as possible. We all collect and gather items that we do not want or need. A friend of mine cannot turn down anything that is cheap or free. Consequently, her home is full of things that she does not need. An acquaintance of mine finally sold some old furniture that she and her husband had been given when they first got married.

"I always loathed it," she says. "It was big and ugly, but it was free. Our house feels so much better now that it's gone."

Clutter can be almost anything that is no longer needed. It makes good sense to get rid of the old, outmoded and unwanted to make room for something new and desirable. Every so often my wife and I have a clean-out at home and toss out all sorts of things that we no longer want. Even though I'm inclined to hoard things, I feel a tremendous sense of release each time we do this.

Clutter in any of the eight areas of the pa-kua creates problems and obstacles. For instance, if the Wealth area of your home is cluttered, you would experience feelings of negativity and confusion concerning your money. Money would be hard to find until the clutter is removed.

Clutter in the Fame area would tend to indicate that you have doubts and confusions about your standing in the community.

Clutter in the Marriage area indicates the potential for problems in your relationship. At the very least, your relationship would not be developing in the way you would wish.

Clutter in the Family area can lead to family disagreements and a desire for individual family members to do things on their own, rather than as a family.

Clutter in the Children area creates worry and uncertainty. It can affect communication between parents and their children.

Clutter in the Knowledge area makes it hard to learn, and difficult to retain what you have learned.

Clutter in the Career area indicates uncertainty about your chosen career.

Clutter in the Mentors area makes it hard to attract the right person to you. You will either find it hard to attract anyone, or will attract the wrong sort of person, until the clutter is removed.

I have been in homes where there is clutter everywhere. You can imagine the difficulties these people experience until they finally gain control of their homes.

Clutter blocks and constricts the beneficial ch'i from spreading easily throughout the home. It is often caused by people's insecurities or fears at letting go. I knew a lady who would not even toss out the daily newspaper once she had read it. When she died, her double garage was full of old, rotting newspapers while her expensive car sat outside exposed to all the elements!

The Good Luck Center

You may be wondering what the center of the pa-kua indicates. This area is known by a variety of names. In the East, it is usually referred to as the **Good Luck** sector. However, it is also known as the Spiritual Center, Soul Center, Ch'i Center, and Happiness Area.

The center of your home needs to be looked after. If it is well tended, you will attract good fortune and luck into your life. You will also experience spiritual growth.

It is often possible to hang a chandelier or crystal in this area of the house. Any attractive lighting fixture will suffice. This attracts beneficial ch'i and reflects it out to every other part of the home. You may not be able to place a chandelier in this position, but activate this area in some way. You will find that your insights and personal growth will be a joy to behold.

A ceiling fan in this position helps to keep the ch'i flowing to every part of the house.

Individual Rooms

The pa-kua can be placed over individual rooms just as over the whole house. Place the bottom side of the pa-kua over the entrance of the room and then check out the eight areas. You may find, for instance, that your bed is placed in the Career area. This may not be a problem, but there is likely to be conflict if, for instance, you are wanting to start a family.

Check for clutter in each area of the room. A friend of mine has a tidy house, but was finding it hard to progress financially. I could find no signs of clutter in the house, which was well-balanced from a feng shui point of view. I puzzled over this for some time, until his wife mentioned that when he undressed for bed he simply dropped all his clothes to the floor in the wealth area, where they stayed until morning. As soon as he started putting the dirty clothes in the laundry and hung up his other clothes before going to bed, his finances improved. In effect, the wealth area in their bedroom was cluttered for some eight hours every day, and this is what was holding my friend back.

Directions and Elements

Each of the eight sides of the pa-kua also indicates a direction and an element. The need for directions may sound surprising when you consider that the pa-kua is laid down using the position of your front door, which could theoretically be facing any one of the eight directions. The compass directions are not used when performing the Aspirations of the Pa-kua. However, they are used inside the house for determining the best rooms for different family members.

South	Fame	Fire	Adult daughter
Southwest	Marriage	Earth	Mother
West	Children	Metal	Youngest daughter
Northwest	Mentors	Metal	Father
North	Career	Water	Adult son
Northeast	Knowledge	Earth	Youngest son
East	Family	Wood	Eldest son
Southeast	Wealth	Wood	Eldest daughter

Nowadays, the traditional family terms are not always appropriate. Consequently, the southwest direction, which is perfect for the mother, could nowadays represent an older woman. Likewise, the adult son could represent any young man, and the eldest daughter could indicate any mature female who lived in the house.

These directions are determined by using a compass inside the door or entrance to the different rooms. A room that has the door opening to the northeast would make a good bedroom for a young boy or the youngest son.

In the East, houses are frequently designed with the front of the house facing to the south to attract as much sunlight as possible. This means that the directions given above also determine the best areas of the house for different activities. For instance, the southeast is the ideal place for a study or office, as this is the wealth area. The south is also a good place for a study, office or workrooms, as it is the fame area. The daughters of the family should use the rooms in the southwest as this area relates to marriage. Young children should use the rooms in the west as this sector relates to them. Older children should use the rooms in the northwest to attract mentors who can help them. Teenage children should use rooms in the north to help them focus on career. The east is a good direction for the master bedroom as this is the family sector.

In traditional feng shui, houses always faced south and the front door and most important rooms faced in this direction, also. The kitchen traditionally faced east, and the rooms of the older members of the family faced southeast.

The Eight Trigrams Method

The Eight Trigrams Method also makes use of the pa-kua. The eight trigrams come from the I Ching[1] and each relates to a different compass direction. This method is sometimes known as the Nine Stars, and is named after the Big Dipper, which indicates the North Star in the northern hemisphere. The Big Dipper consists of just seven stars, but the ancient Chinese added two symbolic, imaginary stars to indicate good and bad omens. Hence, there are the nine stars.

The eight trigrams are made up from three lines that are either broken or complete. There are eight possible combinations, one for each direction of the octagonal pa-kua.

The Individual Trigrams

Chien — The Creative

Direction Northwest

Symbol Heaven

Keyword Strength

Element Sky

Chien consists of three unbroken lines. These lines are known as yang lines. Chien relates to the head of the family, which is usually the father, and the rooms that he is most likely to occupy, such as the study, den, or main bedroom. Chien represents energy, determination and persistence.

K'un — The Receptive

Direction Southwest

Symbol The Earth

Keyword Obedience

Element Earth

K'un consists of three broken lines (known as yin lines), and represents the maternal qualities. Consequently, it usually indicates the mother and the rooms she is most likely to occupy, such as the kitchen and sewing room. K'un symbolizes close relationships, particularly that between husband and wife.

Chen — The Arousing

Direction East

Symbol Thunder

Keyword Progress

Element Wood

Chen is composed of two broken (yin) lines above an unbroken (yang) line. It represents the oldest son. As Chen's direction is in the East, this makes a good position for the oldest son's bedroom. It relates to decisiveness and forward progress.

Sun — The Gentle

Direction Southeast

Symbol Wind

Keyword Pentration

Element Wood

Sun consists of two yang (unbroken) lines over a yin (broken) line. It relates to the oldest daughter. Consequently, her bedroom should be located in the southeast part of the house. It relates to wholesomeness, perception, and inner strength.

K'an — The Abysmal

Direction North
Symbol Water
Keyword Entrapment
Element Water

K'an is made up of a yang line between two yin lines. It relates to the middle son. His bedroom would ideally be in the north side of the house. K'an relates to ambition, drive, and hard work.

Li — The Clinging

Direction South
Symbol Fire
Keyword Magnificence
Element Fire

Li consists of a yin line between two yang lines. It relates to the middle daughter. Her bedroom should be located in the south part of the house. Li relates to happiness, laughter, beauty, and warmth.

Ken — Keeping Still

Direction Northeast
Symbol Mountain
Keyword Pause
Element Earth

Ken is made up of two yin lines beneath a yang line. It relates to the youngest son. His bedroom should be in the northeast part of the house. Ken relates to stability and consolidation.

Tui — The Joyful

Direction West
Symbol Mouth
Keyword Joy
Element Lake

Tui consists of two yang lines beneath a yin line. It relates to the youngest daughter. Her bedroom should be in the west part of the house. Tui relates to pleasure, joy and satisfaction.

Personal Trigrams

Your personal trigram is based on the year of your birth. You can look up your personal trigram in Appendix 2.

Your home also has a personal trigram depending on which direction the back of your home faces. In feng shui, this direction is known as where the back sits. For example, a Tui house faces east, but the back sits to the west.

Name	Back sits	Front faces
Li	South	North
K'un	Southwest	Northeast
Tui	West	East
Chien	Northwest	Southeast
K'an	North	South
Ken	Northeast	Southwest
Chen	East	West
Sun	Southeast	Northwest

The perfect home for you is one where the trigram of the house is the same as your personal trigram. Fortunately, the eight houses can be divided into two groups, the East Four Houses and the West Four Houses. The East Four Houses are Li, K'an, Chen, and Sun. The West Four Houses are Chien, K'un, Ken, and Tui. Each of these form a harmonious grouping based on the cycle of elements. The East Four Houses are made up of the fire, water, and wood elements, and the West Four Houses all belong to the elements of earth and metal.

You are likely to be happy in a home that belongs to the same grouping as you. If you are a Li, for instance, you would be happy living in any of the East Four Houses (Li, K'an, Chen, and Sun). You would also be happy living in a home where the front door opened to the east. Likewise, if you belong to the West Four Houses you would be happy living in a house where the front door faced the west.

An immediate difficulty may have occurred to you. What happens when you belong to, say, the East Four Houses, but your partner belongs to the West group? In the past, the trigram of the man of the house was always the deciding factor. Nowadays, it is usually the trigram of the major breadwinner. Individual rooms are arranged according to the trigram of the person using them most.

It has always been considered extremely fortunate when a husband and wife share the same group of houses. This means that the same directions and positions will be beneficial for both of them.

Positive and Negative Directions

In every home there are four positive directions and four negative ones. These are determined by the way the house sits. For instance, in a Chien house, northwest, northeast, southwest, and west are considered positive directions, while south, southeast, north, and east are considered negative directions. The positive and negative directions for each type of home are shown in Figure 2F (next page).

Each direction refers to a different area of life.

House	Chien	K'un	Ken	Tui	Li	K'an	Chen	Sun
Sitting towards	NW	SW	NE	W	S	N	E	SE
Positive Directions								
1. Prime	NW	SW	NE	W	S	N	E	SE
2. Health	NE	W	NW	SW	SE	E	N	S
3. Longevity	SW	NW	W	NE	N	S	SE	E
4. Prosperity	W	NE	SW	NW	E	SE	S	N
Negative Directions								
5. Death	S	N	SE	E	NW	SW	W	NE
6. Disaster	SE	E	S	N	NE	W	SW	NW
7. Six Shar	N	S	E	SE	SW	NW	NE	W
8. Five Ghosts	E	SE	N	S	W	NE	NW	SW

Figure 2F

Prime Location

The Prime location is a good one. It is always in the same direction as the house sits towards. It is sometimes known as *Fu Wei,* which means "good life." This area is always sited at the back of the house and is a good place for bedrooms.

Health Location

The Health location is a good area that provides energy and good health. It is an excellent location for the master bedroom and the dining room. This area should be stimulated to help anyone suffering from ill health.

Longevity Location

The Longevity location provides peace, harmony, and good health. This area should be stimulated when family life is not going as smoothly as it should be. It can eliminate marital discord and family problems.

Prosperity Location

The Prosperity location is the most positive area in the house. It represents progress, financial success, enthusiasm, and vitality. This area is good for the front door, kitchen door, study, or home office. The Prosperity location is often known as *Sheng Chi,* which means "generating good ch'i." The direction indicated by the Prosperity location is your most fortunate direction. If you can orient the most important things in your life in this direction, while avoiding shars, your success is assured. You can enhance this area by having your bed point in this direction, and by traveling to work in this direction.

Death Location

The Death location is related to accidents, illness, and other misfortunes. It is a good place in the house for the toilet. (In fact, all of the negative directions are good locations for the toilet as this is where bad ch'i is "flushed" away.) This is the worst location in the house and your front door should not face in this direction.

Disaster Location

The Disaster location is related to disputes, legal problems and arguments. It is a good place for storerooms and for the pantry and toilet. Your bed should not be aligned in this direction.

Six Shars Location

The Six Shars location is related to procrastination and loss of reputation and money. This is a good location for the kitchen or toilet.

Five Ghosts Location

The Five Ghosts location is related to fire, theft, and money difficulties. If your front door faces in this direction you are likely to suffer from fire or theft. This location is a good position for storerooms and the toilet.

To determine the exact areas of your home that relate to these locations you need to overlay a pa-kua over a floor plan of your home. You can use either the octagonal form or a square or rectangular version. If your house is an unusual shape, you may have to use two or three pa-kuas to cover the entire house. If you are using the octagonal version, the central position of the pa-kua is placed over the Good Luck area in the center of the house.

Imagine that you live in the house shown in Figure 2G. This is a Chen house, which faces west and sits to the east.

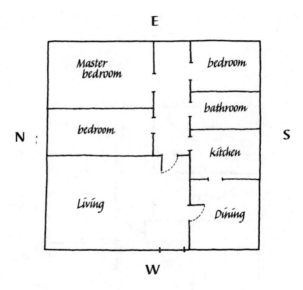

Figure 2G

For ease of explanation, we will use a square-shaped pa-kua that fits over the floor plan of the house (Figure 2H).

This means that the four positive directions are: Prime in the east, Health in the north, Longevity in the south-east, and Prosperity in the south.

Naturally, there are four negative directions as well: Death is in the west, Disaster in the southwest, Six Shars in the northeast, and Five Ghosts in the northwest.

Now that we have this information, we can interpret the results. I usually start with the Prime direction as this is always the same direction that the house sits towards.

In this house, the Prime direction is in the east and takes up part of both the master bedroom and the hallway.

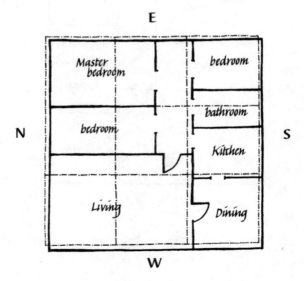

Figure 2H

This location is the perfect site for bedrooms. The Prime location is also known as *Fu Wei* (literally "good life"), and bodes well for the master bedroom. In the East, they believe that if your bedroom is located here you will have more male descendants than female ones. This is good if you happen to be wanting a boy. However, if you are wanting a daughter, you will have to display some items relating to baby girls on your dressing table.

The Health location is situated in the north in this house. This location is considered a good one for the master bedroom and the dining room. We have neither of these in the Health location in this house, but the second bedroom is here, which is almost as good. This is the area of vitality and good health. The occupant of this bedroom will benefit from this.

The Longevity location is in the southeast. This area is taken up with the third bedroom and half of the bathroom. This bedroom is the ideal one for any elderly people living in the house. In China, this area is known as *Nien Yi,* which means "a long life with many heirs." It is unfortunate that half of the bathroom is included in the Longevity location as it means that some of the benefits of this location are being "flushed" down the toilet. A large mirror on the wall that divides these two rooms would make a good remedy for this.

The Prosperity location is in the south and includes the kitchen and half of the bathroom. This direction is usually the most auspicious direction in the whole house. Unfortunately, water gets drained away in both the kitchen and bathroom, making this the worst possible placement for these rooms. These two rooms would need a number of remedies to offset the negative aspects of the bathroom and kitchen. The most important would be to ensure that none of the pipes that drain the water away are visible. Hanging a crystal in both rooms would encourage the ch'i to flow upwards and away from the downpipes. Both rooms should be decorated in cheerful, positive colors to encourage the ch'i to come in and stay for a while.

The Death location suffers from a bad name, and is the first of the negative locations that are present in every house. In China this area is known as *Chueh Ming* ("total catastrophe") and it relates to accidents, illnesses, and other disasters. It is the perfect spot for the toilet.

Unfortunately, in this house the Death location takes up the half of the living room that includes the front door. This is the worst possible place for the front door, because it relates to ill health and loss of money and reputation.

To make matters even more difficult, the other half of the living room is in the northwest, which represents the Five Ghosts location. This relates to fire, theft, and financial problems. Consequently, the living room in this house will need a number of remedies to protect the occupants.

The front door would need to be well-lit and appear attractive to visitors. The chairs where the occupants sit should ideally be in the part of the living room that relates to the Health location, to ensure their vitality and health.

The Disaster location is in the southwest. This area relates to arguments, disagreements, and anger. Unfortunately, the dining room is in this location. A chandelier or other form of bright lighting would be needed in this room to avoid disputes while entertaining guests.

The Six Shars location is in the northeast and incorporates some two-thirds of the master bedroom. Six Shars relates to procrastination, loss, and scandal. Consequently, the bed should ideally be sited in the part of the room covered by the Prime location.

I have deliberately chosen this particular house as many of the positive areas are in negative locations and vice versa. No home is perfect, and you will probably find one or two areas in your own home will be in the wrong locations. There is no need to be alarmed by this. Simply make the necessary remedies, and you will find life going more smoothly for you. (Chapter 11 contains all the feng shui remedies that you will need for any problem area.)

As you can see, both the Aspirations of the Pa-kua and the eight trigrams give us a good picture of the entire house. However, neither gives us all the information we need to provide a complete picture. To do that we have to look at the front door and each of the rooms. We will start on that in the next chapter.

Feng Shui Tips

8. Avoid clutter. Make a concentrated effort to discard anything that you are simply storing and not using.

9. Help your forward progress by activating your home using the areas indicated by the Aspirations of the Pa-kua.

10. Single-level homes produce more ch'i than split-level homes. Split-level homes also confuse the ch'i when it comes in the front door as it does not know whether to head up or down. It is also believed that if your living room is on a higher level than the dining room and kitchen, all the good ch'i will leave the house with your visitors. Bedrooms, studies and recreation rooms also should not be on a higher level than the dining room. Finally, it is considered negative to enter a house on the higher level and then go down some stairs to the rest of the house. This is because going downward signifies a demotion or loss of status.

11. The house should face the south.

12. The front door should face the south.

13. Kitchens should face east.

14. Bedrooms should not open directly onto the kitchen.

15. The ratio of windows to doors should not exceed three to one.

16. Long, straight hallways should be avoided.

17. There should not be three or more doorways in a straight line.

18. Single-level homes are better than split-level homes.

19. Spiral staircases should be avoided.

3

The Front Door

Your front door represents you and your approach to life. We normally come in and out of our front door without noticing anything. It can be an interesting exercise to enter your property and consciously try to see all the things that a stranger would notice when he or she visited. Ideally, we want the front path and front door to be cheerful and welcoming. Consequently, peeling paint on the front door, a bell that does not work, and a door that sticks all create bad feng shui. Plenty of light, flowering plants, and an uncluttered entrance all create good feng shui.

The front door is of supreme importance in feng shui as it is the main location where ch'i enters the house. In feng shui we want the front door to be slightly larger than the back door. This is to ensure that all the beneficial ch'i does not come in through the front door and immediately go out the back door.

The front door should be in proportion to the size of the house. If it is too large, it allows valuable ch'i to escape.

This is believed to cause financial problems. If the door is too small for the size of the house, the amount of ch'i able to come in is restricted (Figure 3A). In the past, large doors were used on castles, churches, and public buildings. They were designed to intimidate and over-whelm everyone who came inside. Presumably, you do not want to do this to your guests, nor do you want financial problems.

The opposite thing happens if your front door is too small. A small door not only constricts the amount of ch'i that can enter, but also tends to make the occupants ner-vous and apathetic.

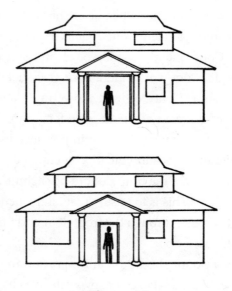

Figure 3A

The front door is the door that is used most frequently in your home. If you always come in and out of your home through a door other than the front door, this door then becomes your main—or front—door.

The front door should ideally be on the left-hand side of the house when you are looking out. Obviously, you have no control over this if you are already living in your home, but it is something to bear in mind next time you move. The dragon looks over the left-hand side of the house, and his energy and bountiful ch'i enters the house more easily when the front door is located on this side. A front door placed in a central position is better than having the door on the right hand side.

Traditionally, the front door should be on the east or south sides of the house. This means that you will be warmed by the morning sun when you leave for work. Consequently, you will start the day in a better mood than you would if your front door was situated in the west or north.

We do not want any shars to affect the front door. This is the single most important aspect of feng shui. The front entrance must be protected. The most serious shar of all occurs when the house is sited on a T-junction, with a street heading directly towards the front door. This is made even worse if this street heads downhill towards your front door.

The path leading towards the front door can also create a shar if it consists of a straight line leading from the road to your front door.

A single tree can create a shar, also, particularly in winter, when the exposed branches can point directly to the front door.

Fortunately, there are remedies for all of these. The street can be made to symbolically disappear by planting a hedge or erecting a fence, so that the street is no longer visible.

The path can be changed to a gentle curve, or perhaps be moved slightly so that it forms a right angle just before the front door.

Additional trees can be planted to remove the negative effects of a single tree. It is best if these are evergreen trees. Alternatively, two lights can be erected on poles, one on each side of the front path between the tree and the front door. This creates a triangular formation, with the point directed away from your front door (Figure 3B).

If none of these remedies can be used, a pa-kua mirror placed above the front door will serve to eliminate the potential harm coming from these shars. A pa-kua mirror symbolically captures the shar and reflects it back where it came from.

The driveway, which is considered part of the front entrance to your home, should not be narrower at the street end than it is at the house; this constricts the ch'i. A light on each side of the driveway makes an effective remedy for this.

The driveway should not slope steeply downhill away from the house as this allows good luck to flow away. A gentle slope does not have the same effect. Ideally, the

Figure 3B

front door will open onto flat land, rather than a hill sloping either up or down. A hill sloping upward symbolizes
obstacles, delays, and frustrations.

Flowers and other plants create additional ch'i when
placed on either side of the driveway. The front garden
needs to be well looked after. Weeds and dead leaves represent lost opportunities, as well as discourage ch'i.

Many homes in cities have an entrance at the top of a
flight of steps leading up from the sidewalk. This creates
good feng shui, as the occupants subconsciously feel safer

raised up and away from the street. It is a good idea, in this instance, to plant shrubs on both sides of the steps to help encourage the ch'i.

It is not good feng shui for your front door to be situated below the street level. This tends to constrict the ch'i and makes the occupants feel unsettled and trapped. The remedy for this is to keep the entrance well lit and have live plants close to the front door.

The main entrance should offer protection from the elements. It is not fun to get drenched with rain while fumbling for your keys. It is also unpleasant for your guests to remain exposed to the elements while waiting for you to open the door.

The entrance should be as inviting as possible. This both encourages ch'i, and creates pleasant expectations in the minds of your visitors. As you know, first impressions are important. If the front door needs painting and there is a collection of shoes and a dead potted plant by the entrance, your expectations go down. If, on the other hand, the entrance looks clean, uncluttered, and welcoming, your guests will immediately feel brighter and more positive about entering your home. Ch'i feels exactly the same.

The front door should be easy to locate. If your guests find it hard to find, the ch'i will find it equally as difficult. We have friends who have a concealed front door on the side of their home. In the front of their house are double doors leading from the living room to their front garden.

Almost every new visitor to the house knocks on these doors, as the front door is so hard to find.

The front door should open in rather than out. Doors that open out discourage ch'i from entering.

The front door should open onto a bright, well-lit room, giving a glimpse of part of the interior of the home. We want the entrance foyer to appear expansive. If the front door opens onto a small lobby area, the ch'i is constricted and confined. The remedy for this is to put up a large mirror. The mirror should be large enough that it does not appear to cut off your visitors' heads. A mirror in this position makes the entrance area appear larger and encourages the ch'i inside. It can be a good idea to place the mirror above a small side-table or other piece of furniture. Fresh flowers or ornaments could be placed on top of this to help attract the ch'i indoors.

The interior should be well-lit to encourage the ch'i to enter. Dimly lit and gloomy entrances discourage ch'i. The remedy for this is to increase the amount of light in the entrance area. A chandelier would be perfect for this, as the crystals energize the ch'i and reflect it in every direction.

It should not be possible to see the back door from the front door. This situation allows the ch'i to enter the house, only to immediately leave again. Also, if the back door is at the end of a long hallway leading from the front door, you have an internal shar. If possible, change the position of the back door. Alternatively, a screen could be put up to conceal the back door from anyone entering the front door. Crystals or wind chimes can be hung up immediately inside both the front and back doors to encourage the ch'i to linger. Finally, if the back door is solid, a mirror can be placed on it to encourage the ch'i back inside.

It is bad feng shui for the front door to open directly onto a staircase going either up or down (Figure 3C). This confuses the ch'i as it does not know whether to go upstairs or into the rooms on the ground floor. It also means that the occupants will be inclined to come into

Figure 3C

the house and immediately go to their own rooms, rather than socialize with other family members. This does not apply if the staircase is at right angles to the front door as this arrangement allows the ch'i time to get used to the layout of the house. The remedy for a staircase that goes directly up from the front door is to hang a crystal from the ceiling above the bottom step. The ch'i will be attracted to this, rather than to the staircase. Usually, a staircase going downstairs from the front door will have a door. Keep this door closed whenever possible.

It is best if your guests see an attractive lobby area or living room when the front door is opened. However, we do not want the door to open directly onto the living room as this destroys the privacy of the occupants. The remedy for this is to partially screen the entrance. A bookcase, decorative screen or large potted plants can provide the necessary privacy without detracting from the feng shui of the room.

If your guests see the kitchen when they first come into the house, they will become preoccupied with food, and the kitchen will become the entertainment area, rather than the living room. They will also tend to eat too much. If you do not want this to happen, keep the kitchen door closed or screened from view.

The front door also should not face the door of a toilet or bedroom. Ideally, we do not want to see the toilet, stove or fireplace from the front door. It is believed that if the front door faces a bedroom the occupants will always feel tired. Conversely, if the front door faces a study, the occupants will be active and industrious. Water relates to wealth in feng shui. Consequently, people with a front door facing the toilet will remain poor as the wealth of the family is continually flushed away.

It can be a revealing exercise to pretend that you are a potential buyer and walk up the drive to your front door, noticing all the things that you no longer see. We all view our homes emotionally, and it is hard to see it with the same eyes that a stranger would use. You may find it helpful to take photographs. Once you are able to see your front entrance dispassionately, you will notice the areas that need painting and cleaning. You will notice a difference in outlook the moment you have made any improvements to your front door. You will feel better, more ch'i will come in, and your guests will feel more welcome. Incidentally, you will also have increased the value of your home for any potential buyer.

As you can see, the placement of the front door is of extreme importance in feng shui. The positions of the front door and the stove are the most important aspects of feng shui in the home.

Feng Shui Tips

20. The size of your front door should be in keeping with the size of your house. If the front door is overly large, compared with the size of the house, your fortunes will suffer. If it is too small, ch'i is constricted and there will be disagreements in the family.

21. Remedy any shars that may be afflicting your front door. This is the most important single aspect of feng shui. Look for angled rooflines of neighboring houses, straight lines, streetlight poles, a single tall tree, and anything sharp, angled, pointed or straight. If your home is facing a T-junction, for instance, you will need to make the road that heads towards your front door "disappear." A pa-kua mirror above the front door will do this. Fences and trees can also create an effective remedy.

22. Prune back trees that conceal the front door. Your front door represents your career, and you need it to be as clear as possible.

23. Make sure that your front door is as welcoming as possible. It should be easy to find and appear to encourage visitors in.

24. Wind chimes, attractive door mats, hanging plants, flower boxes, and statues of animals all encourage ch'i into the front door.

25. If you have a small, constricted entrance, use a large mirror to make the room appear more expansive.

26. Eliminate a straight-line shar from the front gate to the door by placing a bird bath, pond, or fountain near the front door. This will also attract luck and good fortune.

27. The front door should be slightly larger than the back door. This allows the ch'i to flow in quickly and easily, and spend time in the house before flowing out again.

28. The land and buildings on the left side of the front door as you look out should be slightly higher than those on the right. (This is because land and buildings on the left symbolize the dragon. Those on the right symbolize the tiger.)

29. The best position for the front door is on the left side of the house, looking out. This allows the green dragon to protect the main entrance.

30. The front door should not be in a straight line with the back door. This creates a shar, with all the ch'i escaping just as soon as it gets in. It is hard to concentrate in a house like this. Use furniture or mirrors to help guide the ch'i in a curving manner through the house. You can also hang crystals in the rooms between the front and back doors to encourage the ch'i to linger.

31. A solid front door is better than a glass door. If your front door is largely glass, partially cover it with curtains or apply a decorative transfer to it. This is to ensure that neither the ch'i nor your guests accidentally mistake it for a window.

32. If the front door is made of two or more panels, ensure that they are all equal in size. This helps create harmony and balance.

33. It can be a good idea to paint the front door in a contrasting color to the side of the house to emphasize it and to encourage the ch'i.

34. It is a good idea to frame the front doors with trees or shrubbery to give the illusion of privacy. However, it is essential that the front door remains visible.

35. Flowers on each side of the front path encourage ch'i and raise the spirits of your visitors.

36. Try to see your main entrance as if you were visiting it for the first time. Notice all the imperfections, and correct them. You will feel happy with the results and will also feel more ch'i coming into your home.

4

The Kitchen

Some of my earliest memories relate to the kitchen, watching my mother prepare food. I loved watching her practiced efficiency as she prepared the food, and adored the smell of what she produced. Consequently, for me, the kitchen has always represented love, warmth, comfort, and security. Your earliest memories probably relate to the kitchen as well.

Of course, in earlier times the kitchen was the center of the home in many ways, and the family would gather there to talk and keep warm while dinner was being prepared. This is not always the case nowadays, and I know people who never use their kitchen at all, preferring to eat out all the time.

Have you ever noticed how people frequently gather in the kitchen at parties? I have a feeling that this is connected in some way to recapturing the nurturing, comforting, loving feelings from our childhoods.

The kitchen should appear welcoming. It should be light and airy to attract plenty of beneficial ch'i. In this room, in particular, the ch'i should flow as smoothly and as unimpeded as possible. We want the ch'i to enter the freshly prepared food, as this benefits the whole family. Consequently, the kitchen should be well-lit and ideally have windows to let in plenty of natural light.

The stove or oven is traditionally the seat of the family's wealth. The Mandarin word for food is *ts'ai*. This sounds much like the word for wealth. Also, of course, we need food to live. Consequently, next to the front door, the kitchen is the most important part of the house.

The stove should face toward the center of the house (the good luck position). This placement increases the family's prosperity. However, when the stove faces the front door, the health and prosperity of the family suffers.

The stove also should not face the toilet, the door to the master bedroom, a staircase, or a bed.

The person working at the stove (or oven or microwave) should be able to see anyone coming into the room without turning his or her head too far. Consequently, a door behind this person is considered bad. The remedy for this is to place a mirror beside the stove to allow the cook to see anyone entering the room. We do not want the cook to be surprised by someone walking in unexpectedly, because this is believed to have a bad effect on the food.

Incidentally, if you go into the kitchen of a Chinese restaurant, you are likely to find mirrors around the oven.

These mirrors symbolically multiply the amount of food coming out of the oven, which increases the opportunities for making a profit.

There should be sufficient room around the stove for the cook to work. If the cook feels cramped and confined, the quality of the meal can be affected. A remedy for this is to paint the kitchen in a light color and to increase the amount of light in the room.

On the other hand, we do not want the kitchen to consist of a large open space where people continually walk through and distract the cook. If your kitchen often seems to be a main highway, place a table in the middle of the room to act as a barrier. This table can then be used in food preparation and perhaps also serve as an eating area.

The stove should be kept clean and well looked after. If it is not working the way it should, negative ch'i is created. This is not surprising. Because the stove represents the family's wealth, we want everything about it to be working as smoothly as possible.

Consequently, make sure that you regularly use all of the elements or burners on the stove. It is easy to get into the habit of using the same ones every time. Using all of them can help your prosperity.

We also want the larder and refrigerator to be well-stocked with food. This is because the quality and quantity of food available reflects directly on the family's prosperity. A seemingly limitless supply of food symbolizes abundance, contentment, and happiness.

If the house is two or more stories high, we do not want a toilet directly above the kitchen. The toilet creates negative ch'i, which will adversely affect the luck and wealth of the family.

The kitchen should be close to, and on the same level as, the dining room. This is because beneficial ch'i is produced in the kitchen. We want as much of that as possible to reach our family and guests. If the dining room is situated well away from—or on a different level to—the kitchen, much of the ch'i is lost. It is also believed that if the dining room is situated at a higher level than the kitchen your guests will take the beneficial ch'i away with them when they leave.

The stove represents both the fire and metal elements. The refrigerator and sink represent water. Traditionally, fire and water do not mix. However, it is unlikely that you will be preparing your meals over an open fire. The metal of the stove contains the fire, and metal and water get along well. However, it is interesting to note that the oven comprises both fire and metal, which do not get along. Earth provides the balancing element between fire and metal. Consequently, it is a good idea to use earthenware and ceramic pots in the oven.

Despite the fact that the oven is metal and the refrigerator water, they should not be placed side by side. This is because the fire element of the oven, although protected by the metal exterior, is still too close to the water element of the refrigerator. As wood comes between fire and water in the cycle of elements, a wooden table could be placed between these two objects. Alternatively, the wall could be painted green (to represent the wood element). It is better though, to keep the refrigerator and sink well away from the stove.

Incidentally, white is a good color to paint the kitchen as it relates to the metal element. This helps harmonize the different metallic appliances, such as the stove, refrigerator and dishwasher, in the kitchen.

We do not want any pipes or drains to be visible in the kitchen. Water drains away through these, which symbolizes wealth draining away.

We do not want the kitchen to be visible from the front door, unless you want to spend your whole life worrying about food. A screen can effectively conceal the kitchen. Alternatively, wind chimes or a hanging crystal can serve as an effective remedy.

Feng Shui Tips

37. The kitchen should be well lit and have a feeling of spaciousness. As the kitchen symbolizes the family's wealth, it should be well lit to encourage as much ch'i as possible into the room. If it is dark and gloomy, you will not want to spend any time there.

38. The cook should be able to see anyone who enters the room without turning his or her head more than forty-five degrees. If this is not possible, place mirrors to allow the cook to see the doorway.

39. The stove must be kept clean and in good condition, as it relates directly to the wealth of the family.

40. Use all of the elements on your stove as this helps your prosperity.

41. Keep the kitchen well stocked with food to give the impression of abundance.

42. Try to conceal all pipes and drains, as they symbolize wealth draining away.

43. The kitchen should have an airy, spacious, and welcoming feel.

5

The Dining Room

The dining room should seem spacious, comfortable, and welcoming. The atmosphere of this room is almost as important as the food. Time spent in this room should be stimulating and enjoyable. The family should spend happy times here, talking and relaxing, as well as eating.

The dining room should be close to the kitchen, but not close to the front door. If your guests can see the front door from the dining room, they are likely to eat their meals and then leave.

The main focus of the room is the table. Everything else is of lesser importance. The dining table should be placed near the middle of the room, or at least in a position where your guests can get up from the table without feeling restricted by a wall.

Many people who live on their own fall into the habit of always sitting at the same position at the dining room table. However, this is considered negative in feng shui as none of the other chairs are ever used. This means that you are symbolically discouraging any visitors. Make sure that you have at least three chairs around the dining room table, and vary your seating position so that they all get used. This will encourage guests into your home.

The dining room should not be at a lower level than the living room. This is one of the reasons why split-level houses are not favored in feng shui. When the dining room is lower than the living room, it is believed that the beneficial ch'i will flow into our visitors, and then leave the house with them.

Round or oval tables are considered better feng shui than square or oblong ones. There are two reasons for this. Square and oblong tables create shars from the angles at each corner. This is eliminated in many tables by slightly rounding the corners. However, when two people sit across from each other on a square or oblong table it still seems adversarial. King Arthur discovered long ago that a round table was better for communication and is more harmonious than an oblong one. Pa-kua shaped tables (octagonal) are also considered good as they attract energy from all directions.

We do not want too much furniture in this room, particularly if it makes the room appear cramped. It is better to have only the dining table and chairs in this room and enjoy the feeling of spaciousness, than to include sideboards and other furniture that make the room appear small and constricted.

Paintings and mirrors can be used to enhance the ch'i energy. In the dining room, the Chinese often use paintings

of food, or, alternatively, mountain scenes with gently flowing rivers. Mirrors, of course, not only symbolically double
the amount of food on the table but also double the number of friends we have.

The dining room chairs should be comfortable. We do
not want our guests to finish their food and get up
immediately. The family members should sit with their
backs to walls, rather than the windows. This provides
them with plenty of support, which means they can
entertain their guests with greater confidence.

The seating arrangement is an art in itself. The head of
the family should ideally sit facing the main entrance to
the room. Traditionally, the mother and father sat at
opposite ends of a rectangular table. In the past, the
father was always considered the head of the house.
Nowadays, it is usually the person who brings most
money into the household who receives this title. Like
most civilizations, in the past China was a patriarchal system. However, times change, and feng shui has kept pace
with the times, and reflects the world we live in today.
Nowadays, it is considered perfectly acceptable for them
to sit side by side.

We want to encourage ch'i into this room to create a
pleasant environment for the family and friends to eat
and enjoy each other's company. The atmosphere should
be intimate and conducive to conversation. The Chinese
consider food to feed the spirit as well as the body. Consequently, eating should be done in a pleasing environment whenever possible.

Extra ch'i comes into this room if it is located on the corner of the house, with windows on two sides. South has traditionally been considered the best location for the dining room, and it is considered a compliment to your guests to seat them so that they are facing in this direction.

A dining room with two entrances is considered good as this encourages the ch'i to flow. However, it is better if the two doorways are not opposite each other. If they are, the room risks becoming little more than a hallway between different parts of the house.

Overhead beams in the ceiling create overhead shars and should be avoided whenever possible. It is better for any beams to cross the dining table lengthwise. Try not to seat anyone immediately below an overhead beam. One useful remedy for overhead beams is to hang two small bamboo flutes in the middle of the beam.

Many homes do not have a separate dining room. The dining area is frequently part of the living room or kitchen. In these instances, a screen can give the illusion of a separate dining room (Figure 5A). You can also create this illusion with a potted plant. These dividers also allow the ch'i to flow more smoothly and make your guests feel more comfortable.

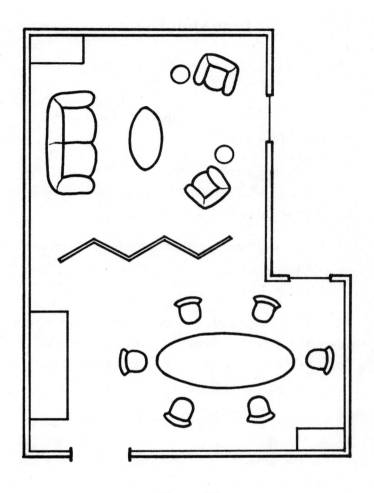

Figure 5A

Feng Shui Tips

44. The dining room should be either a separate room or a clearly defined part of another room.

45. The dining room should not be at a lower level than the living room.

46. The best shaped dining room tables are round, oval or octagonal. Ensure that square and oblong tables have slightly rounded corners.

47. Hang a large mirror in the dining room. This is one of the best rooms in the house for a mirror as it symbolically doubles the amount of food on the table.

48. Do not overcrowd the people sitting at the table with too much furniture. This constricts the valuable ch'i. Avoid clutter. The simpler this room is, the better.

49. Even if you live alone, have at least three chairs around the dining room table. Make sure that you do not sit in the same chair for every meal. If all the chairs are used, you will encourage guests into your home.

6

The Bedroom

We all spend about a third of our lives in our bedrooms. In this room we want to be able to relax and fall asleep easily. Consequently, we want this room to be as comfortable and restful as possible. Naturally, we are at our most vulnerable when we are asleep. Therefore, the bedroom has different feng shui requirements than the other rooms and, in a sense, we need to feel protected and secure in this room.

Square- and rectangular-shaped bedrooms are the best from a feng shui point of view. This shape eliminates the shars caused by irregularly shaped rooms and allows the ch'i to flow smoothly and easily.

There should be just one entrance. When the bedroom has two doors, it is more likely to be used for through traffic and the occupants will not sleep as peacefully.

The ceiling of the room should not be slanted or have exposed beams. Site the bed under the highest part of the ceiling if the ceiling slopes, and attach two bamboo flutes to any exposed beams.

It is important that we allow enough ch'i to enter our bedrooms during the day to sustain us throughout the night. We can do this by allowing as much light as possible into the bedrooms during the day. Sunlight is good, but we do not want direct sunlight on the beds. This is because direct sunlight is believed to over-activate the bed, making it hard to get to sleep.

Bedrooms are also places where we can retreat and spend time on our own, feeling totally safe and protected. We should emerge from our quiet, introspective times feeling revitalized and restored. We need sufficient ch'i to do this.

Bedrooms are often used for a variety of purposes other than sleeping. For instance, many people study in their bedrooms. An acquaintance of mine is writing a novel in his bedroom, as it is the only place where he has room to set up his computer. If this is the case, extra ch'i needs to be encouraged into the room to stimulate the brains of the occupants. A crystal suspended over the desk will activate the ch'i in the immediate area. It is also a good idea to separate the room into specific working and sleeping areas. This is particularly important if exercise equipment is used in the bedroom. To ensure a pleasant sleep you must keep your bed separate from machinery, office equipment, and other items that do not usually belong in a bedroom.

The bed should be placed in a position where the occupants can see anyone coming into the room. Ideally, they should not have to turn their heads more than forty-five degrees to see who is coming in (Figure 6A). Usually, the best position for the bed is diagonally across from the door. A mirror can be used as a remedy to make it easier to see who is coming into the room.

The bed should touch a wall to gain support. The best placement is for the head of the bed to be in contact (Figure 6B, next page) with the wall. If the bed does not make contact with a wall, the occupants are likely to feel unsettled and restless. We do not want the bed to be placed against a window, either. This is because ch'i leaves through the window and you may not receive enough of it during the night if it is all escaping out the window. It is

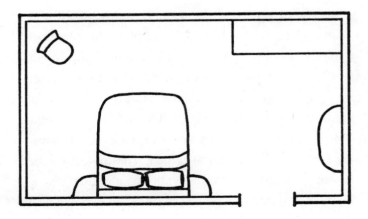

Figure 6A

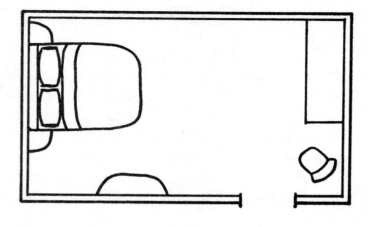

Figure 6B

better to have a small table or chair between the bed and the window.

The foot of the bed should not point directly at the main entrance to the room (Figure 6C). This placement reminds people coming into the room of the "coffin" position. In the past, Chinese people were buried according to their horoscopes. Sometimes this meant they could not be buried for a month after they had died. The coffins were lined up in the courtyards in front of temples waiting for the right day to be buried. The foot of the bed pointing towards the door is reminiscent of this.

The bed should not be placed under an exposed beam (Figure 6D). The person sleeping in this position is likely to experience health problems in the part of the body that

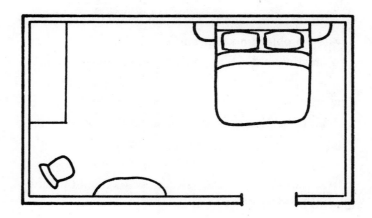

Figure 6C

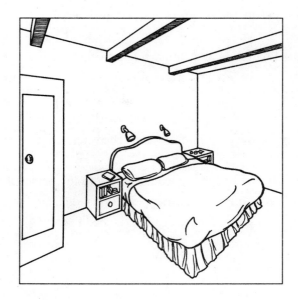

Figure 6D

is lying under the beam. For instance, if the beam crossed over the person's chest, he or she would be likely to develop problems in that part of the body. Beams running lengthwise down the bed are believed to create marital disharmony and ultimately drive the couple apart. However, in some bedrooms there is no choice and the bed has to be placed under a beam. In this instance, it is better if the beam runs lengthwise down the bed, as this does not cause health problems. However, for the sake of marital harmony, the beam should be rectified by hanging two bamboo flutes from it.

Some feng shui practitioners say that the head of the bed should point north. They say that you will benefit from the magnetic force that comes from the North Pole, and consequently sleep better and also be more likely to remember your dreams when you wake. I have experimented with this and found no appreciable difference in the quality of rest I received. All the same, if the layout of the room allows it, it is a good idea to position the head of your bed to face north to follow the natural flows of energy. However, do not be concerned if it is not possible to do this.

In fact, my bed is aligned according to my personal trigram. There are four favorable positions, dictated by your personal trigram, for the head of the bed to face.

Four Favorable Positions
(from most to least restful)

Trigram	Position
K'un	Southwest, northwest, west, northeast
⁓ Ken	Northeast, west, northwest, and southwest
Chien	Northwest, southwest, northeast, and west
⸱ Tui	West, northeast, southwest, and northwest
⸱ Sun	Southeast, east, south, and north
Chen	East, southeast, north, and south
Li	South, north, southeast, and east
K'an	North, south, east, and southeast

Naturally, if two people share the same bed, you may have to compromise on the choice of direction. If you are a K'un, for instance, and your partner is a Ken, the best direction for both of you would be west. Experiment with these, but do not place your bed in an unusual part of the room simply to face the most restful direction. Aesthetics play an important part in feng shui, and it is likely that you have already placed your bed in the correct position intuitively.

The bed should not be moved when the wife is pregnant. This is because the Chinese believe that molecule-sized spirits, known as *ling*, live under the bed waiting to give the unborn baby the breath of life (ch'i). Underneath the bed should not be dusted or cleaned during the pregnancy.

In other rooms, it is impossible to have too many mirrors. However, they should be used sparingly in the bedroom. Mirrors are desirable in the bedroom, but should not be placed directly in front of the foot of the bed. This is because people waking up in the middle of the night might see their reflection in the mirror and think it is a ghost. Also, mirrors in this position put strains on the marriage.

The master bedroom should be sited as far away from the front door as possible. This symbolically makes the occupants feel safer, which means they will sleep better. It also makes sense to situate the bedroom as far away from the noises of the street as possible.

Your bedroom should be a place where you can totally relax. Keep objects that remind you of tasks that need to be done out of the room, or at least out of sight. The first thing you look at when you wake up in the morning should be something pleasant and attractive. You are fortunate if you can wake up and immediately see a beautiful scene outside your bedroom window. If the first thing you see when you wake up is a pile of unwashed laundry, or work that you brought home from the office, you are not going to start the day off nearly as well. Make sure that items like these are not in your immediate view when you wake up.

It is common for houses in the West to have the bedrooms placed in a line along a hallway. The hallway can create a shar, or poison arrow, which points directly at the end room. Also, too many doors opening onto the same passage can create disagreements and frustration.

Ensure that there are no external shars pointing towards the windows of the bedroom. The remedy for this is heavy drapes. However, if they are kept pulled all the time, additional lighting is needed in the room to encourage the ch'i.

Be aware that the door of the room can also create a shar, if the sharp edge points directly at the bed (Figure 6E). To prevent this, make sure that the door is opened fully. You may have to move the furniture around if this shar cannot be eliminated. An alternative remedy is to hang a mirror on the other side of the room to reflect the knife-edge back to the door.

Figure 6E

Other internal shars can arise if the room is irregularly shaped. An L-shaped bedroom, for instance, contains a major shar from the intersection of the two walls pointing across the room. Make sure that the bed is not placed in line with this, as the occupants would ultimately suffer health problems as a result. The remedy is to hang a crystal or set of wind chimes on the ceiling approximately six inches away from the shar. An alternative remedy is to place mirrors on the two walls that create the shar.

Bedrooms are often used as storage areas. This creates clutter which adversely affects the ch'i. Even if the items are placed out of sight, they can still disrupt the flow of ch'i. For instance, objects stored under the bed create negative ch'i that can affect the marital relations of the occupants. It is also believed that you will have dreams about the items stored under the bed.

The correct colors for the carpet and wallpaper in the bedroom relate to the occupant's element. This is particularly the case with children's bedrooms where we want the colors to relate to the element immediately preceding theirs in the cycle of elements.

If the child's element is fire, the correct color is green.

If the child's element is earth, the correct color is red.

If the child's element is metal, the correct color is yellow.

If the child's element is water, the correct color is white.

If the child's element is wood, the correct color is blue or black.

Remedies are required if the color scheme in your child's bedroom clashes with his or her element. Naturally, it is better to change the color scheme, but this can be expensive, particularly if the clashing color happens to be in the carpet.

If the child's element is fire, the clashing colors are black and blue. Add green to the color scheme to remedy this.

If the child's element is earth, the clashing color is green. Add red to the color scheme to remedy this.

If the child's element is metal, the clashing color is red. Add some yellow to the color scheme to act as a remedy.

If the child's element is water, the clashing colors are yellow and brown. Add some white to the color scheme to act as a remedy.

If the child's element is wood, the clashing color is white. Add some blue to the color scheme to act as a remedy.

For adults' rooms we ideally want a mixture of the color relating to their personal element as well as the element immediately preceding theirs.

It is not a good idea to use the room in the far corner diagonally to the right from the front door as a child's bedroom. This is the Marriage sector and is the most powerful position for the master bedroom. If this room is given to a child, he or she will tend to rule the house.

A child's bedroom also should not be outside the pa-kua placed over the design of the house. A room that is out on its own in this way is said to be unprotected. If there is no alternative to this placement, a mirror on the wall adjoining the rest of the house serves to symbolically pull the unprotected room back into the pa-kua.

If your love life needs stimulating, remove all childish toys from the bedroom. These could be teddy-bears, model airplanes, or anything else dating from your childhood years. Remove anything that relates to a previous relationship. Your new partner will not want to see these. Place the bed in such a position that it can be accessed from both sides. Hang a large, round mirror on the wall. Round mirrors are preferred over square or rectangular as the corners could create shars. Remove anything from the room that reminds you of work. It is hard to feel romantic when you are staring at a pile of unwashed laundry.

Children decorate their rooms in exciting, imaginative ways that reflect their current hobbies and interests. Even though you are an adult, you are still allowed to do exactly the same with your bedroom. A bedroom does not have to be boring and purely functional. Allow it to express some of your enthusiasms. You will sleep more contentedly, your dreams will be pleasant, and you will wake up feeling more refreshed in the morning.

Feng Shui Tips

50. The ideal position for the bed is diagonally as far as possible from the entrance to the room.

51. The foot of the bed should not directly face the door to the room.

52. Make sure that you can see anyone coming into the room without turning your head more than forty-five degrees. Use a mirror, if necessary, to enable you to easily see anyone coming in the doorway.

53. The bed should not be placed under a beam. If there is no alternative, it is better for the beam to run the length of the bed, rather than the width.

54. Place the bed against a solid wall, if possible, rather than under a window.

55. A round mirror in the bedroom will enhance your relationship.

56. Do not place a mirror directly in front of the foot of the bed. If you wake up during the night, you may startle yourself by seeing your reflection.

57. The bed should be accessible from both sides if you want to attract a partner into your life.

58. Allow sufficient room under the bed for the ch'i to flow. We want the ch'i to circulate above, below and on at least one side of the bed. If underneath the bed is used as a storage area, you are probably constricting the ch'i and not gaining the full benefit of the bed.

59. Do not place the dressing table directly opposite the door, as this can lead to relationship problems. Dressing tables usually have mirrors which, in this position, reflect the beneficial ch'i in the bedroom, creating apathy and lack of passion for the people using the room.

60. A live plant can stimulate the energy of a bedroom. However, do not have too many plants in this room as they can use up all the available ch'i.

7

The Bathroom

The toilet and bathroom are extremely important rooms in the house as they are places where water (money) drains away. The ch'i should be allowed to flow smoothly into and out of these rooms without impediment. Consequently, overly ornate bathrooms are not good from a feng shui point of view as they tend to hold the ch'i inside the room. In fact, the Chinese prefer relatively simple, functional bathrooms with little in the way of ornaments or other decorations. All the same, you should make this room a pleasant one with delicate colors and one or two objects that you find attractive. A potted plant can also help encourage ch'i into this room. Green and blue colored towels help you to relax, while at the same time encourage the water to flow freely down the pipes. Blue is also a good feng shui color for the bathroom and toilet as it relates to the water element.

Light colors are better than dark ones in the toilet and bathroom. Different shades of blue to represent the water element make a good choice. However, any color works well here, except for red (as water and fire oppose each other). A friend of mine in Phoenix has a white bathroom, but his shower curtain provides some welcome color. It is blue with goldfish swimming all over it. Because it is the only color in the room, you cannot help but notice it. This provides an extremely effective silent affirmation every time the bathroom is used.

The one exception to a simple, purely functional bathroom is when it is located in the marriage sector of your home. If it is located here, make the bathroom as beautiful and as attractive as possible. Display favorite ornaments and hang a crystal from the ceiling to encourage the ch'i. Ideally, the bathroom should have a window to allow light and ch'i to enter. This is because the bathroom is considered a negative location in feng shui. We do not want all the love and romance to be symbolically flushed down the toilet. By enhancing and beautifying this room, we are encouraging ch'i in and effectively remedying what is normally a negative situation.

If the bathroom is located in the middle of the house, in the good luck area, it will send negative ch'i throughout the house. It will also send all your good luck down the toilet. If the toilet is located here, it is known as a "dead" toilet. The remedy for this is to place mirrors on all four walls inside the bathroom, which symbolically make the room disappear. It is also a good idea to place a mirror on the outside of the door to a "dead" toilet.

The other unfavorable locations for the toilet and bath-room are in the southwest, northeast, south, and beside or facing the front door. It is believed that if the toilet and bathroom are placed in the southwest and northeast the occupants' health will suffer. If it is placed in the south, the occupants will squabble and not get along with each other. If it is placed beside or in front of the front door, it is believed that the occupants will get a bad reputation. These are traditional interpretations, and there is a remedy for each of these locations. A mirror on the outside of the door reflects the ch'i away from the toilet and bathroom.

The bathroom also should not be located at the end of a long hallway, as this creates a shar heading directly toward it. This means that the beneficial ch'i that has come in through the front door ends up in the toilet! The remedy for this is to keep the lid down on the toilet and to keep the toilet door closed. It would also be beneficial to place a mirror on the outside of this door to make the room sym-bolically disappear.

Mirrors are necessary inside the bathroom, of course. Avoid mirror tiles though, as they create a netting effect that constricts the flow of money.

Traditionally, the north side of the house is considered the best location for the toilet and bathroom.

The bathroom and toilet should not be placed in the Wealth, Fame, or Career sectors of the house. The Death, Disaster, Six Shars, and Five Ghosts locations are all good places for the toilet.

It is preferable for the toilet and bathroom to be separate rooms. If they are combined, you may be able to separate them with a half wall or screen.

The bathroom needs to be kept clean. Unpleasant smells, leaking taps, windows and doors that stick, and any other problems in this room all create negative ch'i, that can adversely affect the wealth and well-being of everyone in the house.

The water pipes should be concealed, if possible. Exposed pipes allow you to see the water—which equals wealth—drain away. Consequently, this room should not be situated in the north or southeast parts of the house. These are the career and wealth sectors.

Keep the bathroom door shut if this room can be seen from the front door, living room, dining room, kitchen, or anyone lying in bed. A toilet facing the front door is believed to flush away all of the ch'i that enters the house. The Chinese prefer to keep the doors to the toilet and bathroom closed anyway, as a matter of good etiquette. They also keep the lid down on the toilet as they do not like to see their money being flushed away.

Any upstairs toilets and bathrooms should not be situated over the front door or kitchen. Both of these locations are related to family problems. A toilet above the kitchen means that water and waste is flushed directly past the most important room in the house.

En suite bathrooms are not recommended from a feng shui point of view, as they spread negative ch'i out into the bedroom. The remedy for this is to use extractor fans as well as natural ventilation to get the negative ch'i away from the bedroom itself. Ceramic surfaces can also act as a remedy for en suite toilets. It is interesting to note that ceramic surfaces are frequently used in bathrooms and toilets around the world. Perhaps, people subconsciously knew that these surfaces can act as a remedy for negative ch'i.

Naturally, there are remedies for any problems caused by the placement of the toilet and bathroom. A mirror on the outside of the door will remove any problems caused by these rooms facing the front door, or being directly above it.

Feng Shui Tips

61. The toilet should be as inconspicuous as possible.

62. The bathroom and toilet should not open directly on to the door of a main room on the opposite side of the hallway.

63. The bathroom should not be sited at the end of a long hallway.

64. Bathroom and toilet doors should be kept closed.

65. Use a screen or half-wall to separate the toilet and bathroom if they are both in the same room.

66. Toilets should not be placed in the middle of the house. This spreads negative ch'i throughout the house.

67. A toilet should not be sited close to the front door. If it is, negative ch'i from the toilet will clash with the positive ch'i coming into the house.

8

The Living Room

The living room should be welcoming and reflect your personality and interests. You should feel totally relaxed and comfortable in this room, and so should your guests. In many homes the living room is used only on special occasions. In this situation, an important part of the house is not being used properly, with the result that other areas of your life will be constricted. Make this room comfortable and pleasant and use it regularly. If you are not doing this already, you will notice a big difference in the quality of your life as soon as you do.

The ch'i should flow freely through the living room. This encourages the family to spend quality time together. The ch'i also makes your guests feel relaxed and comfortable.

The placement of furniture should also be done to allow the ch'i to flow freely, creating feelings of warmth and companionship in the room. People should be able to move around the furniture freely. L-shaped arrangements of furniture are not good, unless they are in a corner of the room. This is because they create a shar when located in the middle of the room.

The furniture should be arranged with care in the room. If the furniture is placed largely on one side of the room, the room will appear unbalanced and lop-sided. This can lead to feelings of constriction. Anyone sitting in this room will feel vaguely uncomfortable, but not know why. People also feel uncomfortable when they are sitting with their backs to the door. Consequently, chairs and sofas should be arranged so that the people using them do not have their backs to the doors. If your room does not allow this, it is considered good manners to offer your guests chairs that face the door, and sit in one that has its back to the door yourself. Ideally, the head of the house should sit in a chair that faces the main entrance to the room. The people doing the entertaining should not sit with their backs towards a window, as this indicates a lack of support. A solid wall behind them increases confidence and makes them naturally more outgoing and hospitable.

The living room should be close to the front door and on the same level. If the living room is on a lower level to the front door, an effective remedy is to hang a crystal in the center of the room to encourage the ch'i upwards. Potted plants also make an attractive remedy.

Do not place couches or chairs under exposed beams as these overhead shars can be oppressive and create discord. Two bamboo flutes hung from the beam act as a remedy if there is no alternative but to place the furniture under it.

A fireplace creates a central focal point in the room and, in the winter months, creates warmth and cheer. However, it can also allow the ch'i to escape up the chimney. The remedy for this is to hang a mirror over the fireplace to reflect the ch'i back into the room.

In many homes all of the furniture is oriented towards the fireplace. Although this may make good sense in winter, it is better feng shui if at least some of the chairs face each other to encourage conversation. Naturally, the chairs should not be placed so close to the fire that people become too hot. The conversation can also become overheated when this happens.

It is also common to have all the chairs facing the television set. The TV creates positive ch'i in the room, because it produces light and sound, but it can also kill conversation.

The furniture in the room should be a mixture of yin and yang. Consequently, some items should have square corners and others round. Some authorities insist that everything have rounded corners, but this is not practical, and is likely to concentrate people's thoughts on money. It is better to create a harmonious mixture of furniture that you personally find attractive.

The living room should be well-lit, but make sure that the lights are not too strong and harsh. Balance the overhead lights with table or floor lamps to light up different parts of the room. Place a pa-kua over a floor plan of the room to determine the positions that you want to activate.

The wealth sector is particularly strong in the living room. Make sure this sector is well lit to reap the rewards that you deserve. It is also an excellent place for a prized possession, a potted plant, or the television.

You may like to organize your furniture to make the wealth sector the focal point of the room. Other good areas to highlight in this way are the marriage and family sectors. Alternatively, if the room is not large, you may place comfortable chairs in all of these sectors, arranged in such a way as to encourage conversation.

Negative ch'i is created in the living room when two doors directly face each other at opposite ends of the room. If possible, use a screen to hide one of the doors. Alternatively, wind chimes or a hanging crystal by one of the doors act as a remedy. A door and a window opposing each other also create negative ch'i, as do two windows. The remedy is to keep the blinds pulled over one of the windows.

If the opposing doors form a passage that is used all the time, try and arrange the furniture so that entertaining in this room is not affected by people walking through. If the doors are near a wall, a mirror will remove the shar-like effects of the straight line through the room.

The Family Room

A family room should be comfortable and informal. The furniture should be casual and arranged in a way that encourages comfort and communication. This room should also be uncluttered. Family rooms often serve as storage rooms as well. There is no problem with this as long as the items being stored are put away tidily out of sight.

It is likely that the uses this room is put to will change as the family grows. A table-tennis table may be discarded in favor of a billiard table, for instance, as the family grows up.

Each area of this room relates to a different member of the family as shown by the pa-kua. Items belonging to the oldest son, for instance, should be kept in the east. Items belonging to the youngest daughter should be kept in the west, and so on. Clutter in different parts of the room will relate to complications in the life of the person affected by that direction.

Feng Shui Tips

68. The most commanding position in the living room is diagonally across the room from the main door. This is the best position for the head of the house, as it means that he or she is in control.

69. Gloomy areas in the living room adversely affect the area of life indicated by the Aspirations of the Pakua. Use floor or table lamps where necessary to spread the light throughout the living room.

70. Arrange the furniture evenly around the living room. If too much furniture is placed on one side of the room it appears unbalanced, and that side can feel weighed down and constricted.

71. Arrange the furniture so that people can move freely around the room without feeling as if they are undertaking an obstacle course.

72. The backs of chairs or sofas should not face any entrances to the living room. People sitting in these positions feel insecure and lacking in support.

73. The living room should feel comfortable and welcoming. This is helped if you have comfortable chairs and sofas, sufficient light and pleasant pictures or ornaments at which to look.

74. Your guests will feel more positive when facing south or east. Sunlight makes them more enthusiastic and conversation.

9

Color in Your Home

The powerful effects that different colors create have been known for thousands of years. Primitive humans used colors to ward off evil and to increase luck and virility. The ancient Chinese used colors as symbols to represent the different seasons. Green symbolizes wood and represents spring. Red symbolizes fire and represents summer. Yellow and orange symbolize the sun casting its warming glow on the earth; they represent the end of summer. White symbolizes metal and represents autumn. Blue symbolizes water and represents winter.

Colors have both positive and negative effects upon us. Faber Birren, a color psychologist, reported that normal people tend to find favorable qualities in different colors, but neurotics are more likely to notice the unfavorable.[1]

We all react to color whether we are aware of it or not. Imagine sleeping in a bright-red bedroom or cooking a meal in a jet-black kitchen. Colors provide the emotional tone to the room. Some colors excite us, others make us

angry. Still others calm us down. An interesting experiment was done some years ago when violent prisoners
were kept in cells that had been painted pink. This color
drained the inmates' aggression, and they became model
prisoners. As this experiment shows, color can have dra-
matic effects, so we need to be careful with what colors
we choose and how we use them.

In feng shui, colors control and assist reflected light.
The combination of color and light should provide the
best possible conditions to live in. It is best to choose your
color schemes in the rooms themselves, as colors have a
habit of changing when looked at under different types of
lighting. Warm lights, for instance, make warm colors
appear even warmer, while cool lights do the opposite.

Naturally, you should have the colors relating to the
different elements of the people living in your home, but
you should have a variety of other colors simply because
you like them. Be careful not to have opposing colors,
though. For instance, too much red would not be a good
choice for you if you belong to the water element, as fire
and water do not harmonize.

Choose the colors of your ceilings carefully. Light colors are generally better than dark. Dark colored ceilings
remind the Chinese of dark rain clouds overhead. Dark
colors also prevent the ch'i from rising. Consequently, the
ch'i does not circulate the way it should and your wealth,
health, and good luck can all be affected.

Softer colors are ideal for the bedroom. Any color that makes you feel peaceful and relaxed is ideal here. Pink, peach, cream, ivory, beige, tan, and light green are warm and gentle. Avoid strong colors, such as red and orange in the bedroom.

Earth colors, such as yellow, orange, brown, and green, are suitable for the kitchen. Avoid blue in this room as it relates to the water element. In fact, speaking generally, blue is not good as the dominant color in any room (except the bathroom, as mentioned in Chapter Seven), as it tends to make people introspective and quiet. It is also inclined to make people feel cold. I have been in living rooms where a very light blue worked, but it is a difficult color to experiment with. It is better to introduce blue in the form of throw rugs, paintings, ornaments, or other objects.

Light and pastel colors can be used to make small rooms appear larger. Red, yellow, and blue do the opposite and decrease the size of rooms. Good use of light colors can brighten up a dark corner. A well-lit, sunny part of the house can be painted in light or dark colors. Hot colors, such as red, create stimulating environments. Conversely, cool colors, such as blue, are restful and encourage quieter activities.

These are, of necessity, very general guidelines. Use the colors that you personally like. It is important that the colors in your home reflect you and your feelings.

Most of the time these will also create good feng shui in your home.

It is best to start designing a room by choosing one color to be the dominant color in the room. Choose another color for the carpet or furnishings. Add a third color to either harmonize your first two colors together, or to create a contrast. This method is simple, but effective.

Colors and the Pa-kua

The five elements can be used in conjunction with the Aspirations of the Pa-kua to determine which colors can be used to enhance different areas of your home.

When the pa-kua is overlaid on top of the cycle of the five elements, with earth being placed in the center, we receive an interesting mixture of colors that can prove extremely useful.

Wealth area   Green, red, violet, and blue

Fame area   Red, green, and yellow

Marriage area   Red, pink, and white

Family area   Green, red, and blue

Children area   White and gold

Knowledge area   Black, green, and blue

Career area   Black, white, and green

Mentors area   White and black

You can use these color schemes in the areas of the house that relate to the pa-kua, or alternatively keep objects of these colors in the relevant areas.

Here are the general meanings of the different colors to help you choose the right colors for you and your home.

Red

Keywords   Exciting, energetic

Red is the strongest color of all. It is not commonly found in nature, and, when we do see it, it gives a strong message. In China, red has always been considered a color of happiness and prosperity. It is a highly auspicious color. In the East brides still wear red to attract good luck from heaven, and eggs that have been dyed red are distributed one month after babies are born.

Red is inspirational, exciting, and dynamic. It can give enormous confidence. About twenty years ago, a friend of mine was appointed manager of a large shopping mall, the first woman to be appointed to such a position. She was a controversial choice at the time, but quickly proved that she was the perfect person for the job. After she had been in charge for a few months, the owners asked her to give a speech to the managers of all the other shopping malls in the group telling them what they should be doing to improve their results. My friend was terrified at the prospect, as she never spoke in public and was being asked to address a group of people who had all violently opposed her appointment. I suggested that she wear a little bit of red to give her confidence. She bought herself a red suit and matching shoes, and gave a dynamic address that impressed everyone. She had never worn red before, but has done so ever since. Nowadays, she calls red the "color of power."

Red can also be the color of rage. It is passionate and fiery and can create havoc when not used wisely. Red relates to the fire element.

Red should be used in rooms that involve activity and excitement. A recreation room or a home gymnasium are good examples. Red increases physical activity and passion. However, it can also induce insomnia when used in a bedroom.

Orange

Keywords   Aspiration, sociable

Orange is a social, sociable color with considerable drive and energy. It is slightly more reserved than red, being good-natured and likable, rather than passionate. Orange relates to the earth element.

Orange creates some of the excitement of red, but is softened by the yellow. This makes it a useful color in rooms where people meet and talk. Interestingly, orange is also mentally stimulating and is a good choice for study areas, too.

Yellow

Keywords Positiveness, optimism

Yellow is the color of the sun, which casts its life-giving power over us all. Yellow is cheerful, stimulating, and brightening. It provides mental stimulation, which is why it is often associated with gaining wisdom. It can enliven the most gloomy of rooms. In ancient China, it was considered the color of laughter. Yellow relates to the earth element.

Yellow has always been regarded as a mentally stimu-lating color, making it useful in rooms where study or creative activities take place. Do not overdo the yellow, though, as too much of this color can cause headaches. Yellow lifts the feeling of a room and makes people feel happy and joyful, making it a good choice for rooms used for entertainment purposes.

Green

Keywords Peace, tranquillity

Green is right in the middle of the color spectrum, and is the color of nature. It provides feelings of peace, har-mony, and tranquillity. It soothes and restores the soul. In China, green is considered the color of peace and long life. It also relates to spring, with the new begin-nings and growth that are associated with it. Green relates to the wood element.

Green is restful and peaceful, making it a good color for any room used for relaxation and sleep. Green soothes the mind and eliminates tensions and anxieties.

Blue

Keywords Optimism, security

In ancient China, blue symbolized blessings from heaven. It is the color of the sky. Today, it relates to thoughtfulness, constancy, and the truth. It is calming, introspective, and responsible. Blue relates to the water element.

Blue is tranquil and inward-looking. Blue might be a good choice if you have a special room where you go to meditate. Darker blues, such as indigo, aid spirituality and intuition.

Different shades of blue can be effective in the bathroom and toilet. This is because blue relates to the water element. A friend of mine has a highly distinctive bathroom incorporating several shades of blue. It creates an extremely powerful effect.

Violet

Keyword Spirituality, high ideals

Violet uses the energy of red, combined with the optimism of blue, to create a restful color that evokes a sense of wonder. It is not surprising that bishops wear purple robes, as violet has a strong association with the spiritual side of life. This color encourages creativity, idealism, and mysticism.

Violet can be inspirational and fill the mind with dreams of what may be. It is not a good choice for rooms used for entertainment, but can be useful in rooms where concentration is required.

Gold

Keywords Dignity, money

In imperial China, only the emperor and his immediate family were allowed to wear gold robes. Consequently, gold is still believed to attract honor and fame. Gold is positive and optimistic, like yellow, but is considerably more dignified. In the East it is often combined with red to represent good luck and wealth. Gold relates to the metal element.

White

Keywords Purity, brightness

The white of a bride's gown represents purity and innocence. In the martial arts, people with a white belt are "innocent," because they are just beginning. White is basically the absence of color. It creates a love for detail and represents a mind free of cares. It is interesting to note that white is a funeral color in the East. However, it also relates to light, which attracts ch'i, something very

desirable in feng shui. All the same, in the East, they usually offset the white with another "living" color. White
relates to the metal element.

Black

Keywords   Intensity, formality, sophistication

Black absorbs all colors. It is the color of night. It is hard
to relax in rooms that are starkly black and white. It is
often considered gloomy, but in fact it can create a
dynamic, determined approach to problem-solving. Black
relates to the water element. In the West, black is often
considered a negative, even evil, color. However, in feng
shui, black relates to money, and consequently can be a
highly positive color.

You need to be confident to use black as part of the
color scheme in your home. Black and white make a
powerful combination that usually works better in an
office environment than in the home. However, if you are
wanting to make a statement, black can work well in the
living room, hallways, and bathroom. Use it sparingly for
maximum impact.

All colors are either yin or yang, and as you know, we are happiest when we achieve a balance of yin and yang in our home. Red, orange, yellow, and black are yang, and green, blue, and white are yin. Purple can be either yin or yang, depending on the combination of red and blue. If there is more red than blue, it is yang, and, conversely, when there is more blue than red, it is yin. Yin and yang colors can be used together to create balance, but ideally should each be of the same strength.

Sensitive Colors

Black and red are the two most sensitive colors in feng shui. Traditionally, black should not be used on gates, doors, and walls that face north or south. Red should not be used on gates, doors, and walls that face east or west. It is believed that bad luck will come to the occupants of homes that break these rules.[2] Black and red should always be used with great caution.

Feng Shui Tips

75. Color stimulates and energizes ch'i. Bright colors attract ch'i and make the area more stimulating. Red, in particular, is useful as it has always been considered the color of good luck and wealth.

76. Avoid too much of the same color. If the floor, walls, and ceiling are all painted the same color, the result can be restricting and ultimately depressing.

77. Color energizes. Experiment with exciting and different colors, such as red, yellow, and purple, in areas that are used for conversation. Stimulating colors help provide scintillating conversation.

78. By experimenting with the intensity, purity, and brightness of different colors, you can make each room feel perfect for its purpose.

79. Imaginative use of lighting will help you make the most of your color scheme. Try a mixture of strong and soft lighting in each room and notice the effect it has on you and your guests.

80. **Fire People:** Wood relates well to fire. Consequently, green is a good color for you. However, water destroys fire. This means you should avoid black and blue. Earth drains fire. Avoid brown and yellow.

81. **Earth People:** Fire relates well to earth. Consequently, red is a good color for you. However, wood destroys earth. This means you should avoid green. Metal drains earth. Avoid white and gold.

82. **Metal People:** Earth relates well to metal. Consequently, beige, orange, and brown are good colors for you. However, fire destroys metal. This means you should avoid red. Water drains metal. Avoid black and blue.

83. **Water People:** Metal relates well to Water. Consequently, black and blue are good colors for you. However, earth destroys water. This means you should avoid orange and brown. Wood drains water. Avoid green.

84. **Wood People:** Water relates well to wood. Consequently, black and blue are good colors for you. Metal destroys wood. This means you should avoid white and gold. Fire drains wood. Avoid red.

10

Numbers in Feng Shui

Feng shui began with the tortoise crawling out of the Yellow River some five thousand years ago. The markings on its shell formed the basis of feng shui, the I Ching, Chinese astrology, and Chinese numerology. The magic square on the tortoise's back contained all the numbers from one to nine. Consequently, numbers have always been an integral part of feng shui.

Every number has a meaning that can be looked at in a number of different ways. If your house number is 2368, for instance, each of the numbers could be looked at individually, or they can all be added together and reduced down to a single digit. In the West, it is standard for numerologists to pay more attention to the final result of adding all the numbers up and reducing them to a single digit. In the East it is more common to evaluate each separate number.

Numbers are divided into yin and yang. Even numbers are yin and odd numbers are yang. Yang numbers are considered to be more favorable that yin numbers, but balance is required. Consequently, it is better for your house number to contain both yin and yang elements than to be either all yin or all yang.

You may have noticed that Asian people like the number eight. This is because the Cantonese word for "eight" sounds like "prosperity." They also like the number two as it sounds like "easy." However, they dislike number four as it sounds like "death." If your house number is 24, they would interpret this as "easy death." All of this is because the Chinese use homophones to help determine the meanings of numbers. If the number sounds like something pleasant or desirable, it is considered good. This is the reason why number eight is so positive and four is negative. Traditionally, number four relates to the positive traits of love, sex, and education.[1] Here are the homophonic interpretations for each number:

One sounds like "honor." It also sounds like "won."

Two sounds like "easy."

Three sounds like "growth."

Four sounds like "death."

Five sounds like "nothing."

Six sounds like "wealth."

Seven sounds like "sure."

Eight sounds like "prosperity."

Nine sounds like "long life."

Naturally, house numbers usually contain more than one number, and homophones are also used here. The number twenty-eight, for instance, sounds like "easy money." Fifty-eight does not fare nearly as well as it sounds like "no wealth." Forty-eight, even though it contains the number four, is still a good number as it sounds like "much wealth." You would expect four and eight to represent "death wealth," but, in fact, it is a positive combination. This is because four also represents hard work. Consequently, forty-eight means great wealth through hard work and effort.

A friend of mine in Taiwan has a house number of four. He obtained permission to change it to 4B, and made the "B" look much like an eight on his letter box. He told me that his fortunes improved as soon as he made the change. He also still seems to be receiving his mail! This friend told me of someone who lived in number fourteen doing the same thing. "Fourteen" sounds like "surely die" in Cantonese.

Not surprisingly, certain numbers are worth big money as personalized number plates around the world. In Hong Kong, the Transport Department began auctioning license-plate numbers in 1988. In its first year, number "8" sold for $650,000, still a record according to the *Guinness Book of World Records*. The proceeds of these auctions go to charity, and the owners of the license plates can keep them until they die, when the plates are auctioned off again.

The license plate "2828," which means "easy money, easy money," sold for more than $63,000.[2] Incidentally, if you visit Hong Kong, see if you can stay in Room 2828 on the 28th floor of your hotel. You will have to book well ahead to get this room, but your stay will be an extremely pleasant one!

The standard numerological interpretations of each number bear little relationship to the homophonic ones:

> **One** represents independence and attainment.
>
> **Two** represents tact, diplomacy and close relationships.
>
> **Three** represents creativity and expressing the joys of life.
>
> **Four** represents limitations, restrictions, and slow and steady progress.
>
> **Five** represents travel, change, and variety.
>
> **Six** represents service and home, and family responsibilities.
>
> **Seven** represents analysis, spirituality, and growing in knowledge and wisdom.
>
> **Eight** represents money and power.
>
> **Nine** represents love and completion.[3]

If your house number is 2457, for instance, life in your home would be tactful and loving (two), but also restrictive in some ways (four). There would be plenty of variety (five) and you would gradually grow in knowledge and wisdom (seven).

You can also total the four numbers and reduce them down to a single digit. For example, 2 + 4 + 5 + 7 = 18, and

1 + 8 = 9. Nine is the number of love and completion. It also represents good luck and future prosperity. It sounds as if life in this home would be pleasant for the most part, even though you would feel hemmed in and restricted at times.

The nine numbers also relate to colors, elements, and directions and can be used to represent any of these when required. Here are the numbers and colors that relate to each element:

Direction	Number	Color	Element
North	1	Blue, black	Water
South	9	Red	Fire
East	3, 4	Green	Wood
West	6, 7	White	Metal
Center	2, 5, 8	Yellow	Earth

If desired, this can be taken still further to include all eight directions as well as the center:

Direction	Number	Color	Trigram	Element
North	1	Black	K'an	Water
Southwest	2	Yellow	K'un	Earth
East	3	Green	Chen	Wood
Southeast	4	Green	Sun	Wood
Center	5	Yellow	—	Earth
Northwest	6	White	Chien	Metal
West	7	White	Tui	Metal
Northeast	8	Yellow	Ken	Earth
South	9	Red	Li	Fire

Some authorities suggest that you arrange the numbers on your letter box in an uphill progression, saying that this will encourage the ch'i to rise. This is a good idea, except when the final number is a four. Arranging the numbers in this way tends to put most significance on the final number. If the final number of your house number is a four, arrange the numbers in a straight line to place equal emphasis on each number.

Numbers play only a small role in feng shui. However, they can make a big difference as to how easy or hard it is to sell a house. Some years ago, a developer in the city I live in built several identical houses in a new subdivision. Number eight was the first to sell and number four was the last. Even more interesting though, is that although the houses were identical, the developer was forced to sell number four at a loss, simply to get it off his hands. The others all sold for good prices.

Feng Shui Tips

85. If you are choosing a new home, try to buy one with both yin and yang numbers as part of the street address.

86. Arranging the numbers on your letter box so that each number is placed slightly higher than the one before is a good idea, except when the final digit is a four.

11

Feng Shui Remedies

As you no doubt realize by now, there is a feng shui remedy for virtually any problem. This is fortunate, as I have yet to see a house that is perfect from a feng shui point of view. In fact, it is impossible to achieve perfection.

Recently, I was taken to see a home that had been designed according to feng shui. It faced south and was on a bluff surrounded by water on three sides. The house had been built to take advantage of the magnificent harbor views and had large windows opening out on to sun-drenched decks. The developer was extremely proud of what he had achieved and advertised the property as being "feng shui perfect." In fact, for many people it would be perfect. However, it was not the perfect home for anyone belonging to the fire element. There was far too much water for these people, and the constant sunlight coming through the huge windows would provide far too much mental stimulation.

Different Types of Remedies

There are three different types of remedies that can be used. The first involves channeling the ch'i by allowing it to flow freely throughout the house. This involves avoiding or removing clutter and allowing the ch'i sufficient room in which to circulate.

We can also use harmony and balance as a way of curing problems. For instance, a lamp in the garden can serve symbolically to complete an L-shaped house. By doing this, we provide balance and correct something that is seen to be incomplete.

Finally, the most common cure is to add something, such as a mirror or crystal to alleviate a problem. Color can also be used in this manner.

The most common cure involves increasing the amount of light to attract the ch'i. This can be done by using mirrors, crystals, chandeliers, and additional lighting. A light makes a good remedy for a missing corner created by an irregularly shaped room. Objects that reflect light can also be used. Inside our front door we have a collection of glass and crystal ware that is used to encourage the ch'i into our home. All the glass attracts and reflects light, adding to the ch'i. We also keep the lights on inside the front door most of the time to attract ch'i into what would otherwise be a dark entrance.

Chandeliers are wonderful for attracting ch'i and reflecting it out again. The Fame, Marriage, and Knowledge areas all benefit enormously when a chandelier is placed in these parts of the house. A chandelier in the center of the house (Good Luck sector) also benefits the entire home.

Mirrors are possibly the most useful feng shui cure of all. They can be used to symbolically remedy an irregular shaped room. They can deflect shars back where they came from. Mirrors placed at intervals along one wall of a long, straight hallway deflect the ch'i and remedy the negative effects of the shar. Mirrors can add life to any dark or constricted areas of your home. Mirrors can also attract beautiful exterior views into the house. They can make small rooms appear to be twice their size. They can multiply the amount of food on the dining room table. Ideally, mirrors should be as large as possible. Small mirrors tend to symbolically chop off people's heads and feet.

Eight-sided mirrors, in the shape of a pa-kua, are considered extremely powerful and effective. This is because they represent all eight directions. The living room and hallway are good places for this sort of mirror. Ideally, these mirrors should be as large as possible.

An effective place for a mirror is at the top of a staircase, or on the landing. In this position, they stop the ch'i from flowing down the stairs too quickly. Another advantage of a mirror in this position is that you will see a friendly face every time you go up or down the stairs. Smile at yourself every time you go past. After all, a friendly smile creates good ch'i.

Mirrors, like anything else, work best when they are looked after. For the best results, make sure that your mirrors are kept clean and free of dust.

Incidentally, shiny pots, silver trays, and anything else that has a reflective quality can serve as a mirror for feng shui purposes. Sometimes you may not want to hang up a mirror for some reason. An acquaintance of mine was bothered by a shar coming from his next door neighbor's house. He felt that if he hung up a pa-kua mirror to send the shar back, his neighbor would also hang one up starting a "mirror war." He solved the problem by using shiny metal supports on a downpipe on the side of his house. They acted as a hidden mirror to send the shar back, and it was not noticed by his neighbor.

Music and other sounds can also be used. Wind chimes are extremely effective as they not only attract ch'i, but also become an affirmation every time you hear them. The pleasing sounds they make reminds you that the ch'i is flowing. Wind chimes can be metal, wood, or ceramic. Metal wind chimes are extremely useful in activating the Children, Career, and Mentors areas of your home. Bamboo wind chimes are especially useful in the Fame, Family, and Wealth sectors. Metal wind chimes should not be hung in the Family or Wealth sectors as these areas represent the wood element and metal, of course, chops wood.

Wind chimes can be used both indoors and outdoors. Placed outside the front door, wind chimes will double the amount of ch'i that comes in. This is particularly useful if your front door opens on the shaded side of the house.

You can even hang wind chimes in areas where the wind will never cause them to make sounds. You can activate them yourself whenever you go past. Each time you do this, the pleasant sound will attract ch'i and prosperity into your home. I once visited a home which had a large xylophone on display inside the front door. Everyone who came into the house was encouraged to play a few notes to create, attract, and enhance the ch'i.

An aunt and uncle of mine used a large, resonating dinner gong to summon the family to meals. The sound spread throughout their large home attracting ch'i as well as calling the family to dinner. Today, in China, wealthy people keep antique gongs in glass cases to symbolize the preservation and perpetuation of wealth from generation to generation. These are generally kept in the dining room to symbolize an abundance of food.[1]

I have a string of bells in my office. The pleasant sounds they make keep me stimulated and happy. They also remind me that the ch'i is flowing and spreading throughout my office. Bells make an excellent remedy. I hung mine up to increase the ch'i flowing into my office, but they are also believed to be good for the health of the occupants.

Even radio and television sets create and attract ch'i with their light and sounds. The human voice can also do the same. If you hum and sing around your home, you will increase the amount of ch'i available to you. A child practicing the piano or violin will also attract ch'i. I had to remind a friend of this when she complained to me about the constant din her son made whenever he practiced on the drums!

Live objects attract ch'i. Household pets have been proven beneficial in reducing stress and in keeping old people alive and healthy. We all feel better when caring for living things, be they plants or animals. Pets also help circulate ch'i energy. Aquariums containing fish serve as silent affirmations of wealth and prosperity, and also attract ch'i. In Hong Kong almost every apartment contains a fish bowl. Fish symbolize a successful career, and also create an abundance of beneficial ch'i, particularly if the aquarium is oxygenated.

Plants act in much the same way as live animals. A home without any plants at all feels unsatisfying and tends to separate us from nature. Plants are welcoming and give life to empty spaces. Indoors they symbolize nature, and outdoors they attract ch'i toward the house. Freshly cut flowers also attract ch'i into the home. However, they need to be looked after. Sick and dying plants create negative ch'i. At the first signs of ill health the plants need to be attended to or removed. Artificial flowers work just as well as real ones, as long as they are kept dusted and looked after. Dried flowers create negative ch'i, because all the water has been removed. They symbolize death and should be avoided. Live flowers have a highly beneficial effect on the Marriage, Family, and

Mentors areas of the home. Plants that have thorns or prickles, such as roses and cacti, are better kept outdoors where they symbolize protection. A potted plant or hanging plant can encourage ch'i to any area of the house that you wish to activate.

Plants can be placed in front of potential shars, such as protruding corners and sharp angles from furniture.

Water, in the form of an aquarium, fountain, or swimming pool all attract and encourage ch'i. Fountains of moving water create ch'i. Nowadays, it is possible to get small, indoor fountains that are decorative as well as ch'i producing.

Statues or pictures of animals can make useful remedies. Statues of wild animals, such as lions, outside your front door serve to symbolically protect your home. Heavy statues represent stability and courage. Indoors, it is usually better to have more peaceful animals. For instance, a ceramic tortoise makes an attractive ornament and also symbolizes longevity.

Colors can be used as remedies to provide elements that are lacking in different parts of the home. Lighter colors can be used to attract light into certain parts of the house. Any color can be used as long as it appeals to you. For instance, black is usually considered to be a negative color. However, it relates to water, which can be interpreted as money. Consequently, use it if you feel it will serve your purpose. Your choice of colors should relate to the personal elements of the people living in the house.

This means, for instance, that black (relating to water) would be the worst color for someone of the fire element to choose.

Bamboo flutes make excellent remedies, particularly to offset the effect of overhead beams. They are also believed to discourage thieves and to attract good friends. The flute symbolizes peace, tranquillity and contentment. Two flutes are used together. They should be suspended on red ribbons, with the mouthpieces facing downward, for best effect.

Feng Shui Tips

87. Do not hang a mirror opposite any door. This effectively stops the ch'i from entering the next room, and encourages negative ch'i to build up.

88. Keep your mirrors clean. Dust and dirt reduce the effectiveness of mirrors.

89. You cannot have too many mirrors in your home. However, use them sparingly in the bedroom, or any other area that needs to be restful and soothing.

90. Mirrors in the dining room symbolically double the amount of food on the table. They also double the feelings of well-being and enjoyment that you and your guests will experience in this room.

91. A large, octagonal-shaped mirror represents all eight directions and is a powerful force of energy. Place it in the living room or in a hallway.

92. A mirror at the top of a staircase or on the landing prevents the ch'i from flowing down the stairs too quickly. It also means that you will see a welcoming face every time you go up the stairs.

93. Use pa-kua mirrors to send back shars from outside your property.

94. Wind chimes and other objects that create pleasant sounds make useful remedies. They are particularly useful for remedying background noises, such as air-conditioning units or the refrigerator.

95. Table and floor lamps create comfortable pools of light that can illuminate dark areas and encourage more ch'i into any areas that need activating.

96. Plants help the ch'i to circulate and can also be used to hide shars. They add color and create harmony and contentment.

97. Water, particularly moving water, attracts ch'i and money. Consider placing a small ornamental fountain or aquarium in your Wealth location.

98. Live animals help the ch'i to circulate. They also provide love and happiness, which help create harmony and contentment.

12

Conclusion

Now that you have read this book you will find examples of good and bad feng shui everywhere you go. Recently, my wife and I attended a wedding reception at a local hotel. I was interested to find a fountain playing outside the main entrance and a pa-kua symbol created in the patterns of the tiles leading up to the front entrance. Two stone lions stood guard outside these doors. When we walked inside, we found ourselves looking at a large, round mirror with a gold frame. All of these things were new since our last visit. It was just another sign that feng shui has come of age and is being accepted throughout the world.

About ten years ago, a friend of mine who is a property developer decided to use feng shui principles in all of his projects. This was not because he believed in feng shui; it was done purely because he thought it might help him sell more properties to Asian buyers. He was surprised to find that his properties sold better than ever before to people of all nationalities and races. This was because his buildings were harmonious and felt pleasant to prospective buyers. My friend is no longer skeptical, and last time I visited him he was feeding the eight gold and one black fish in his aquarium. This combination of fish means "money, money, money, and protection." The water in the aquarium represents money. The gold of the goldfish also represents money. There are eight goldfish and, as you know, number eight means money, also. Finally, the black fish is in the aquarium for protection. Whenever a fish dies, it is a sign that some disaster has been averted. Naturally, my friend would replace any dead fish right away.

If you were to visit my wife and me in our home, you would find that we have made it as comfortable as possible by using the ideas explained in this book. We found that our family life improved as soon as we made some simple adjustments.

Now it is up to you. Start by making one or two minor changes in your own home. Wait for a week or two to see what changes you notice, and then make a few more. Over a period of time you will notice the quality of your life improving. Friends will comment on how warm and friendly your home is. They may even mention beneficial changes in you and members of your family. If they ask for an explanation, tell them something about feng shui. Achieving harmony and balance in your life is fantastic, but it is a special privilege to be able to introduce it to the lives of your friends. You will be able to give them good advice and tell them where to buy books on the subject.

Back in the 1960s when I was first introduced to feng shui, it was rare to find anyone else who knew anything about it. Today, most people have heard of it, and many know some of the basic principles. I hope that you will carry on with your studies in the fascinating subject. May I wish you a lifetime of bounteous ch'i and good feng shui.

Feng Shui Tips

99. Start by removing clutter. Do this before using any other feng shui remedies.

100. Make any changes slowly and wait for a while to see what effects they cause. Only then should you make another change.

101. Enjoy the changes that feng shui brings to your life. As you start moving toward a life filled with contentment and abundance, you will understand why feng shui is sometimes known as "the art of happiness."

Appendix 1

Elements and Signs for the Years 1900 to 2000

Element	Sign	Year
Metal	Rat	Jan. 31, 1900 to Feb. 18, 1901
Metal	Ox	Feb. 19, 1901 to Feb. 7, 1902
Water	Tiger	Feb. 8, 1902 to Jan. 28, 1903
Water	Rabbit	Jan. 29, 1903 to Feb. 15, 1904
Wood	Dragon	Feb. 16, 1904 to Feb. 3, 1905
Wood	Snake	Feb. 4, 1905 to Jan. 24, 1906
Fire	Horse	Jan. 25, 1906 to Feb. 12, 1907
Fire	Sheep	Feb. 13, 1907 to Feb. 1, 1908
Earth	Monkey	Feb. 2, 1908 to Jan. 21, 1909
Earth	Rooster	Jan. 22, 1909 to Feb. 9, 1910
Metal	Dog	Feb. 10, 1910 to Jan. 29, 1911
Metal	Boar	Jan. 30, 1911 to Feb. 17, 1912
Water	Rat	Feb. 18, 1912 to Feb. 5, 1913
Water	Ox	Feb. 6, 1913 to Jan. 25, 1914
Wood	Tiger	Jan. 26, 1914 to Feb. 13, 1915

Wood	Rabbit	Feb. 14, 1915 to Feb. 2, 1916
Fire	Dragon	Feb. 3, 1916 to Jan. 22, 1917
Fire	Snake	Jan. 23, 1917 to Feb. 10, 1918
Earth	Horse	Feb. 11, 1918 to Jan. 31, 1919
Earth	Sheep	Feb. 1, 1919 to Feb. 19, 1920
Metal	Monkey	Feb. 20, 1920 to Feb. 7, 1921
Metal	Rooster	Feb. 8, 1921 to Jan. 27, 1922
Water	Dog	Jan. 28, 1922 to Feb. 15, 1923
Water	Boar	Feb. 16, 1923 to Feb. 4, 1924
Wood	Rat	Feb. 5, 1924 to Jan. 24, 1925
Wood	Ox	Jan. 25, 1925 to Feb. 12, 1926
Fire	Tiger	Feb. 13, 1926 to Feb. 1, 1927
Fire	Rabbit	Feb. 2, 1927 to Jan. 22, 1928
Earth	Dragon	Jan. 23, 1928 to Feb. 9, 1929
Earth	Snake	Feb. 10, 1929 to Jan. 29, 1930
Metal	Horse	Jan. 30, 1930 to Feb. 16, 1931
Metal	Sheep	Feb. 17, 1931 to Feb. 5, 1932
Water	Monkey	Feb. 6, 1932 to Jan. 25, 1933
Water	Rooster	Jan. 26, 1933 to Feb. 13, 1934
Wood	Dog	Feb. 14, 1934 to Feb. 3, 1935
Wood	Boar	Feb. 4, 1935 to Jan. 23, 1936
Fire	Rat	Jan. 24, 1936 to Feb. 10, 1937
Fire	Ox	Feb. 11, 1937 to Jan. 30, 1938
Earth	Tiger	Jan. 31, 1938 to Feb. 18, 1939
Earth	Rabbit	Feb. 19, 1939 to Feb. 7, 1940
Metal	Dragon	Feb. 8, 1940 to Jan. 26, 1941
Metal	Snake	Jan. 27, 1941 to Feb. 14, 1942
Water	Horse	Feb. 15, 1942 to Feb. 4, 1943
Water	Sheep	Feb. 5, 1943 to Jan. 24, 1944
Wood	Monkey	Jan. 25, 1944 to Feb. 12, 1945

Wood	Rooster	Feb. 13, 1945 to Feb. 1, 1946
Fire	Dog	Feb. 2, 1946 to Jan. 21, 1947
Fire	Boar	Jan. 22, 1947 to Feb. 9, 1948
Earth	Rat	Feb. 10, 1948 to Jan. 28, 1949
Earth	Ox	Jan. 29, 1949 to Feb. 16, 1950
Metal	Tiger	Feb. 17, 1950 to Feb. 5, 1951
Metal	Rabbit	Feb. 6, 1951 to Jan. 26, 1952
Water	Dragon	Jan. 27, 1952 to Feb. 13, 1953
Water	Snake	Feb. 14, 1953 to Feb. 2, 1954
Wood	Horse	Feb. 3, 1954 to Jan. 23, 1955
Wood	Sheep	Jan. 24, 1955 to Feb. 11, 1956
Fire	Monkey	Feb. 12, 1956 to Jan. 30, 1957
Fire	Rooster	Jan. 31, 1957 to Feb. 17, 1958
Earth	Dog	Feb. 18, 1958 to Feb. 7, 1959
Earth	Boar	Feb. 8, 1959 to Jan. 27, 1960
Metal	Rat	Jan. 28, 1960 to Feb. 14, 1961
Metal	Ox	Feb. 15, 1961 to Feb. 4, 1962
Water	Tiger	Feb. 5, 1962 to Jan. 24, 1963
Water	Rabbit	Jan. 25, 1963 to Feb. 12, 1964
Wood	Dragon	Feb. 13, 1964 to Feb. 1, 1965
Wood	Snake	Feb. 2, 1965 to Jan. 20, 1966
Fire	Horse	Jan. 21, 1966 to Feb. 8, 1967
Fire	Sheep	Feb. 9, 1967 to Jan. 29, 1968
Earth	Monkey	Jan. 30, 1968 to Feb. 16, 1969
Earth	Rooster	Feb. 17, 1969 to Feb. 5, 1970
Metal	Dog	Feb. 6, 1970 to Jan. 26, 1971
Metal	Boar	Jan. 27, 1971 to Jan. 15, 1972
Water	Rat	Jan. 16, 1972 to Feb. 2, 1973
Water	Ox	Feb. 3, 1973 to Jan. 22, 1974
Wood	Tiger	Jan. 23, 1974 to Feb. 10, 1975

Wood	Rabbit	Feb. 11, 1975 to Jan. 30, 1976
Fire	Dragon	Jan. 31, 1976 to Feb. 17, 1977
Fire	Snake	Feb. 18, 1977 to Feb. 6, 1978
Earth	Horse	Feb. 7, 1978 to Jan. 27, 1979
Earth	Sheep	Jan. 28, 1979 to Feb. 15, 1980
Metal	Monkey	Feb. 16, 1980 to Feb. 4, 1981
Metal	Rooster	Feb. 5, 1981 to Jan. 24, 1982
Water	Dog	Jan. 15, 1982 to Feb. 12, 1983
Water	Boar	Feb. 13, 1983 to Feb. 1, 1984
Wood	Rat	Feb. 2, 1984 to Feb. 19, 1985
Wood	Ox	Feb. 20, 1985 to Feb. 8, 1986
Fire	Tiger	Feb. 9, 1986 to Jan. 28, 1987
Fire	Rabbit	Jan. 29, 1987 to Feb. 16, 1988
Earth	Dragon	Feb. 17, 1988 to Feb. 5, 1989
Earth	Snake	Feb. 6, 1989 to Jan. 26, 1990
Metal	Horse	Jan. 27, 1990 to Feb. 14, 1991
Metal	Sheep	Feb. 15, 1991 to Feb. 3, 1992
Water	Monkey	Feb. 4, 1992 to Jan. 22, 1993
Water	Rooster	Jan. 23, 1993 to Feb. 9, 1994
Wood	Dog	Feb. 10, 1994 to Jan. 30, 1995
Wood	Boar	Jan. 31, 1995 to Feb. 18, 1996
Fire	Rat	Feb. 19, 1996 to Feb. 6, 1997
Fire	Ox	Feb. 7, 1997 to Jan. 27, 1998
Earth	Tiger	Jan. 28, 1998 to Feb. 15, 1999
Earth	Rabbit	Feb. 16, 1999 to Feb. 4, 2000
Metal	Dragon	Feb. 5, 2000

Appendix 2

Personal Trigram for Year of Birth

Chien

Male: 1913, 1922, 1931, 1940, 1949, 1958, 1967, 1976, 1985, 1994
Female: 1919, 1928, 1937, 1946, 1955, 1964, 1973, 1982, 1991

Tui

Male: 1912, 1921, 1930, 1939, 1948, 1957, 1966, 1975, 1984, 1993
Female: 1911, 1920, 1929, 1938, 1947, 1956, 1965, 1974, 1983, 1992

Continued on page 148.

Personal Trigram for Year of Birth (continued).

Li

Male: 1910, 1919, 1928, 1937, 1946, 1955, 1964, 1973, 1982, 1991

Female: 1913, 1922, 1931, 1940, 1949, 1958, 1967, 1976, 1985, 1994

Chen

Male: 1916, 1925, 1934, 1943, 1952, 1961, 1970, 1979, 1988, 1997

Female: 1916, 1925, 1934, 1943, 1952, 1961, 1970, 1979, 1988, 1997

Sun

Male: 1915, 1924, 1933, 1942, 1951, 1960, 1969, 1978, 1987, 1996

Female: 1917, 1926, 1935, 1944, 1953, 1962, 1971, 1980, 1989, 1998

K'an

Male: 1918, 1927, 1936, 1945, 1954, 1963, 1972, 1981, 1990, 1999

Female: 1914, 1923, 1932, 1941, 1950, 1959, 1968, 1977, 1986, 1995

Ken

Male: 1911, 1920, 1929, 1938,
1947, 1956, 1965, 1974,
1983, 1992
Female: 1918, 1921, 1927,
1930, 1936, 1939, 1945,
1948, 1954, 1957, 1963,
1966, 1972, 1975, 1981,
1984, 1990, 1993, 1999

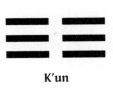

K'un

Male: 1914, 1917, 1923, 1926,
1932, 1935, 1941, 1944,
1950, 1953, 1959, 1962,
1968, 1971, 1977, 1980,
1986, 1989, 1995, 1998
Female: 1915, 1924, 1933,
1942, 1951, 1960, 1969,
1978, 1987, 1996

Notes

Introduction

1. Master Lam Kam Chuen, *Feng Shui Handbook* (London: Gaia Books Limited, 1996. New York: Henry Holt and Company, 1996), 60.

Chapter 1

1. A large collection of yin and yang opposites can be found in *The Key to it All. Book One: The Eastern Mysteries* by David Allen Hulse (St. Paul: Llewellyn Publications, 1993), 350–351.

Chapter 2

1. The *I Ching* can claim to be the oldest book in the world. The concept of yin and yang dates back some

five thousand years. Yin was related to a broken line and yang a straight line. There are four possible combinations of these. By adding another line it was possible to double this and create eight trigrams. These trigrams are what we use in feng shui. In the I Ching, two trigrams are placed, one on top of the other, to create sixty-four hexagrams.

Chapter 9

1. Faber Birren, *Color in Your World* (revised edition Collier Books, New York, 1978. Originally published by Macmillan Publishing Company, Inc., New York, 1962), 10.

2. Albert Low, *Feng Shui: The Way to Harmony* (Malaysia: Pelanduk Publications, 1993), 67.

Chapter 10

1. Richard Webster, *Feng Shui for Beginners*, 77.

2. "Avoiding Bad Luck." Article in the *Miami Herald*, Miami, June 27, 1997.

3. For further information on the meanings of the numbers see *Chinese Numerology: The Way to Prosperity and Fulfillment* by Richard Webster (St. Paul: Llewellyn Publications, 1998) and *Talisman Magic* by Richard Webster (St. Paul: Llewellyn Publications, 1995).

Chapter 11

1. Lillian Too, *Feng Shui* (Malaysia: Konsep Lagenda Sdn Bhd., 1993). 159.

Glossary

Ch'i — Ch'i is the universal life force that is found in every living thing. In feng shui it is often referred to as "the dragon's breath." It is encouraged into the home to give the occupants health, happiness, and prosperity.

Compass School — There are two main schools of feng shui. The compass school uses the person's date of birth and a compass to determine the best locations and houses for people to live in.

Feng Shui — Feng shui literally means "wind and water." It is the art of living in harmony with the earth. If we do that, we will live lives of happiness, contentment, and abundance. Feng shui has been practiced in the Far East for five thousand years. It has now spread around the world and is more popular than ever.

Five Elements — The ancient Chinese believed that everything was created from five basic elements: wood, fire, earth, metal, and water. Each element has its own distinct characteristics and their different combinations play an important part in feng shui. Chinese astrology also uses the five elements and believe that we all contain most, or all, of the five elements in our makeup.

Form School — The form school is the original form of feng shui. It looks at the geography of the landscape and evaluates it for the quality and quantity of ch'i energy available.

Magic Square — A magic square consists of a series of numbers arranged in a grid where all the horizontal, vertical and diagonal rows all add up to the same total. It was the magic square found in the markings of a tortoise that marked the birth of feng shui, the I Ching, Chinese astrology, and Chinese numerology.

Pa-kua — The pa-kua is frequently seen hanging over the entrances to Chinese homes as a protection. It is octagonal in shape and usually has either a yin-yang symbol or a mirror in the center. Around this are placed the eight trigrams of the I Ching.

Remedies — Remedies, or cures, are the different methods used to eliminate the effects of shars or imbalances in the five elements. A hedge or fence used to block out a shar caused by a street heading directly towards your front door would be a remedy.

Shars — Shars, often known as "poison arrows," are negative energies that travel in straight lines. A long, straight hallway inside a house would be a shar, as would be the angle caused by the corner of a neighboring house that pointed directly at your home. There are remedies available for almost all possible shars.

Trigrams — There are eight possible combinations of straight and broken lines that can be formed from three lines. The straight lines are known as yang lines and represent male energy. The broken lines are yin lines and represent female energy. The eight trigrams that are formed in this way represent the eight different points of the compass, and describe the types of houses that face these directions.

Yin and Yang — Yin and yang represent the opposites in Taoist philosophy. Examples would be front and back, night and day, and male and female. Yang is male, and yin is female. Neither can exist without the other. Originally, yin and yang referred to two sides of a mountain. Yin depicted the shady, northern side, and yang described the sunny, southern side.

Bibliography

Chuen, Master Lam Kam. *Feng Shui Handbook*. London: Gaia Books Limited, 1996 and New York: Henry Holt and Company, 1996.

Lagatree, Karen M. *Feng Shui: Arranging Your Home to Change Your Life*. New York: Villard Books, 1996.

Lin, Jami. *Contemporary Earth Design: A Feng Shui Anthology*. Miami: Earth Design Incorporated, 1997.

Rossbach, Sarah. *Feng Shui: The Chinese Art of Placement*. New York: E. P. Dutton, 1983.

Rossbach, Sarah. *Interior Design with Feng Shui*. New York: E. P. Dutton, 1987.

Simons, T. Raphael. *Feng Shui Step by Step*. New York: Crown Trade Paperbacks, 1996.

Thompson, Angel. *Feng Shui: How to Achieve the Most Harmonious Arrangement of Your Home and Office.* New York: St. Martin's Griffin, 1996.

Too, Lillian. *Feng Shui.* Malaysia: Konsep Lagenda Sdn Bhd., 1993.

Webster, Richard. *Feng Shui for Beginners.* St. Paul, MN: Llewellyn Publications, 1997.

Wong, Eva. *Feng-Shui: The Ancient Wisdom of Harmonious Living for Modern Times.* Boston: Shambhala Publications, Inc., 1996.

Index

FENG SHUI FOR BEGINNERS
Successful Living by Design
Richard Webster

Not advancing fast enough in your career? Maybe your desk is located in a "negative position." Wish you had a more peaceful family life? Hang a mirror in your dining room and watch what happens. Is money flowing out of your life rather than into it? You may want to look to the construction of your staircase!

For thousands of years, the ancient art of feng shui has helped people harness universal forces and lead lives rich in good health, wealth and happiness. The basic techniques in *Feng Shui for Beginners* are very simple, and you can put them into place immediately in your home and work environments. Gain peace of mind, a quiet confidence, and turn adversity to your advantage with feng shui remedies.

1-56718-803-6
240 pp., 5 ¼ x 8, photos, diagrams, softcover   **$12.95**

ASTRAL TRAVEL FOR BEGINNERS
Transcend Time and Space
with Out-of-Body Experiences
Richard Webster

Astral projection, or the out-of-body travel, is a completely natural experience. You have already astral traveled thousands of times in your sleep, you just don't remember it when you wake up. Now, you can learn how to leave your body at will, be fully conscious of the experience, and remember it when you return.

The ability to astral travel can change your life. You will have the freedom to go anywhere and do anything. You can explore new worlds, go back and forth through time, make new friends and even find a lover on the astral planes. Most importantly, you will find that you no longer fear death as you discover that you are indeed a spiritual being independent of your physical body.

1-56718-796-X, 256 pp., 5³⁄₁₆ x 8, softcover   **$9.95**

SPIRIT GUIDES & ANGEL GUARDIANS
Contact Your Invisible Helpers
Richard Webster

They come to our aid when we least expect it, and they disappear as soon as their work is done. Invisible helpers are available to all of us; in fact, we all regularly receive messages from our guardian angels and spirit guides but usually fail to recognize them. This book will help you to realize when this occurs. And when you carry out the exercises provided, you will be able to communicate freely with both your guardian angels and spirit guides.

You will see your spiritual and personal growth take a huge leap forward as soon as you welcome your angels and guides into your life. This book contains numerous case studies that show how angels have touched the lives of others, just like yourself.

- Learn the important differences between a guardian angel and a spirit guide
- Invoke the Archangels for help in achieving your goals
- Create your own guardian angel from within
- Use your guardian angel to aid in healing yourself and others
- Enhance your creativity by calling on angelic assistance
- Find your life's purpose through your guardian angel
- Use your spirit guides to help you release negative emotions
- Call on specific guides for nurturing, support, fun, motivation, wisdom
- Visit your guides through past-life regression

1-56718-795-1, 368 pp., 5³⁄₁₆ x 8, softcover   **$9.95**

REVEALING HANDS
How to Read Palms
Richard Webster

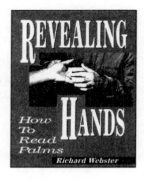

Palmistry has been an accurate tool for self-knowledge and prediction for thousand of years. The ability to read palms can lead you to a better understanding of yourself, as well as the complex motivations of other people. Guide and advise others in a sensitive and caring manner, determine compatibility between couples, and help people decide what type of career suits them best.

Revealing Hands makes it is easier than ever to learn the science of palmistry. As soon as you complete the first chapter, you can begin reading palms with confidence and expertise. Professional palmist and teacher Richard Webster leads you step-by-step through the subject with clear explanations and life-size hand drawings that highlight the points being covered. He provides sample scripts that can serve as a foundation for your readings for others, and he answers all of the questions he has been asked by his students over the years. Whether you are interested in taking up palmistry professionally or just for fun, you will find the information in this book exceptionally entertaining and easy to use.

0-87542-870-3, 304 pp., 7 x 10, 117 illus., softcover $14.95

OMENS, OGHAMS & ORACLES
Divination in the Druidic Tradition
Richard Webster

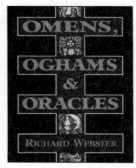

Although hundreds of books have been written about the Celts and the druids, no book has focused exclusively on Celtic divination—until now. *Omens, Oghams & Oracles* covers the most important and practical methods of divination in the Celtic and druidic traditions, two of which have never before been published: an original system of divining using the druidic Ogham characters, and "Arthurian divination," which employs a geomantic oracle called druid sticks.

Even if you have no knowledge or experience with any form of divination, this book will show you how to create and use the 25 Ogham fews and the druid sticks immediately to gain accurate and helpful insights into your life. This book covers divination through sky stones, touchstones, bodhran drums and other means, with details on how to make these objects and sample readings to supplement the text. Beautiful illustrations of cards made from the Oghams, geomantic figures and more enhance this clear and informative book, which also includes chapters on the history, lives and philosophy of the Celts and druids.

Many Celtic divinatory methods are as useful today as they were 2,000 years ago—make modern forms of these ancient oracles work for you!

1–56718–800–1, 224 pp., 7 x 10, softcover   **$12.95**

To order, call 1-800-THE MOON
Prices subject to change without notice

DOWSING
FOR BEGINNERS

The Art of Discovering Water,
Treasure, Gold, Oil, Artifacts
Richard Webster

This book provides everything you need to know to become a successful dowser. Dowsing is the process of using a dowsing rod or pendulum to divine for anything you wish to locate: water, oil, gold, ancient ruins, lost objects or even missing people. Dowsing can also be used to determine if something is safe to eat or drink, or to diagnose and treat allergies and diseases.

Learn about the tools you'll use: angle and divining rods, pendulums, wands—even your own hands and body can be used as dowsing tools! Explore basic and advanced dowsing techniques, beginning with methods for dowsing the terrain for water. Find how to dowse anywhere in the world without leaving your living room, with the technique of map dowsing. Discover the secrets of dowsing to determine optimum planting locations; to monitor your pets' health and well-being; to detect harmful radiation in your environment; to diagnose disease; to determine psychic potential; to locate archeological remains; to gain insight into yourself, and more! *Dowsing for Beginners* is a complete "how-to-do-it" guide to learning an invaluable skill.

1-56718-802-8
256 pp., 5¼ x 8, illus., photos, softcover   **$12.95**

CHINESE NUMEROLOGY
The Way to Prosperity
& Fulfillment
Richard Webster

This book goes back to the very beginnings of numerology, to a time when people thought gods lived in turtle shells, and when the discovery of a tortoise containing a perfect magic square in its markings was an event of national importance. *Chinese Numerology* teaches the original system of numerology which is still practiced throughout the East, and from which Chinese astrology, feng-shui and the I Ching were all derived.

Chinese numerology as presented here is the quickest and easiest method of character analysis ever devised. Right away, you will be able to build a complete picture of a person just as soon as you know his or her birthdate. By the end of the book, you will be able to erect and interpret numerology charts in three different ways. You will know more about yourself and the motivations of others. You'll also know when to move ahead and when to hold back in different areas of your life. *Chinese Numerology* is the first book in the West to explain and teach the traditional Chinese system:

• Draw a numerology chart in a matter of seconds and be able to interpret it accurately

• Is this a money year? A good year to get married? Discover the future trends in you life by looking at your personal years, months and days

• Uncover your compatibility with another person using an easy technique that has never been published before

Includes solar-lunar conversion tables to the year 2000

1-56718-804-4, 260 pp., 7 x 10   **$12.95**

To order, call 1-800-THE MOON
Prices subject to change without notice

TEA LEAF READING
William W. Hewitt

There may be more powerful methods of divination than tea leaf reading, but they also require heavy-duty commitment and disciplined training. Fun, lighthearted, and requiring very little discipline, tea leaf reading asks only of its practitioners an open mind and a spirit of adventure.

Just one cup of tea can give you a 12-month prophecy, or an answer to a specific question. It can also be used to examine the past. There is no regimen needed, no complicated rules to memorize. Simply read the instructions and look up the meanings of the symbols!

Tea Leaf Reading explains the how it works, how to prepare the cup for reading, how to analyze and read tea leaf symbols, how to interpret the symbols you see. It provides an extensive glossary of symbols with their meanings so you can begin interpretations immediately; it provides an index, with cross-references for quick location of the symbols in the glossary; and it has an appendix of crystals and metals that can aid you in reading tea leaves and in other pursuits.

0-87542-308-6, 240 pp., mass market   **$3.95**

MOTHER NATURE'S HERBAL
Judy Griffin, Ph.D.

A Zuni American Indian swallows the juice of goldenrod flowers to ease his sore throat ... an East Indian housewife uses the hot spices of curry to destroy parasites ... an early American settler rubs fresh strawberry juice on her teeth to remove tartar. People throughout the centuries have enjoyed a special relationship with Nature and her many gifts. Now, with Mother Nature's Herbal, you can discover how to use a planet full of medicinal and culinary herbs through more than 200 recipes and tonics. Explore the cuisine, beauty secrets and folk remedies of China, the Mediterranean, South America, India, Africa and North America. The book will also teach you the specific uses of flower essences, chakra balancing, aromatherapy, essential oils, companion planting, organic gardening and theme garden designs.

1-56718-340-9
448 pp., 7 x 10, 16-pg. color insert, softcover   **$19.95**

THE PATH TO
GOOD FORTUNE
The Meng
Lily Chung, Ph.D.

Wouldn't you like to uncover the order of the cosmic flow and how it will affect your luck each day? For thousands of years, the Chinese have done just that with a technique that surpasses any means currently available: The Meng. Meaning *life*, or *destiny*, the Meng brings together the factors of time, place and action to help you chart your future course. The Meng contains some of the most basic components of Chinese philosophy, is part of the lore of Chinese astrology, and makes use of Feng Shui and the I Ching. It puts the wisdom of the I Ching into formulas, enabling you to chart out your life with little effort.

This book is the only guide in the English language for beginners who want to grasp this fascinating tool. The methodology of the Meng enables you to derive a full account of yourself: endowments, strengths, limitations, and the key events of your entire lifetime. Ultimately, it will lead you to the fundamental force which accounts for your outlook and most of your achievements.

1-56718-133-3, 288 pp., 6 x 9, softcover   **$14.95**